REVENUE ENGINE

WHY REVENUE PERFORMANCE MANAGEMENT IS THE NEXT FRONTIER OF COMPETITIVE ADVANTAGE

Steven Woods

Alex Shootman

Revenue Engine

© 2011 by New Year Publishing, LLC
144 Diablo Ranch Ct.
Danville, CA 94506 USA
http://www.newyearpublishing.com

ISBN 9781935547266
Library of Congress Control Number:

PRE-FOREWORD

If you read no other section of this book, turn to Chapter 10 "The Revenue Engine As Strategic Imperative."

Go ahead, read it. Skip this foreword if you have to.

Still here? Then allow me to explain myself.

A couple of years back my colleague and Chief Technology Officer, Steven Woods, published *Digital Body Language*. The book was groundbreaking. In it Steven explained how traditional sales and marketing process had been flipped on its head. Prospects now controlled the tempo and stages of the buying process, and organizations needed to learn how to let go and engage. By reading a buyer's *Digital Body Language* sales and marketing teams learned what actions and behaviors served as road signs in a buyer's journey.

Digital Body Language represented a collective "Aha!" moment for the B2B industry. But when I would meet with CEOs from a variety of businesses and hand them a copy, all too often they would say, "Thanks! I'll pass this on to to my marketing team."

No doubt, any Marketer would benefit from the lessons and case studies Steven highlights in his previous book. And in fact, many marketers did as DBL hit the Amazon bestseller's list. But *Digital Body Language* wasn't just about marketing. It's all about growing revenue. And for any CEO, regardless of sector or size, revenue is job number one.

Ask almost any CEO what his or her board of directors judges them by and they'll share the same answer, "Revenue." In fact, a CEO's goal is simple: grow revenue. But we know implementation is never that easy. We are expected to experiment with different ways of generating revenue, eliminate choke points, expand pipeline, cut out what doesn't work, do more of what does—oh yeah, and do it as cheaply as possible.

In this book, Steven and Eloqua's Chief Revenue Officer, Alex Shootman, explore and explain the moves fast-thinking—and fast-growing—companies have implemented to tremendous results. In Chapter 10, Steven and Alex summarize the practices they've painstakingly laid out throughout the book and bring it to a boil. Together, they've cracked the code to true revenue performance.

In short, this is not a book about marketing. It's not about sales. This is a book about the only thing that matters. Revenue.

So if you still haven't turned to Chapter 10 yet, do it now. It's ten pages that could dramatically change your business.

Joe Payne, CEO, Eloqua

FOREWORD

A revolution is going on, with or without you.

The ubiquity of the Internet, and the subsequent rise of social media, has blurred the imagined lines between marketing and sales. Not only that, it has obscured the distinctions between buyers and sellers.

We are all buyers and sellers now. Prospects and companies alike are acting as publishers. Customers can be your most feared critics or your surest lead to future clients. Feedback is solicited through a variety of instantaneous forums. And even as sales cycles lengthen, the expected wait time for a business's response is an ever demanding "Now!"

For those in sales and marketing, the technological advancements of the last ten years have resulted in a fundamental paradigm shift. In his previous book, *Digital Body Language*, Steven Woods explained how rapidly evolving Web 2.0 tools—from social media to search engines—were flipping the traditional sales and marketing process on its head. Buyers had turned the tables on organizations long accustomed to leading prospects through the education process. Easy access to information irreversibly transformed the market into a buyers' playground.

It's a kind of radical transition that rings alarm bells. But rather than scare, Steven sought to inform. Reading a buyer's *Digital Body Language* provided unprecedented insight into what actions and behaviors led to prospects becoming buyers, and how continuing to engage turned clients into lifetime partners. He introduced tools that make it possible for executives to understand what generates results, and eliminate what doesn't.

Into this new era of accountability steps *Revenue Engine*. In this groundbreaking book, Steven and co-author, Alex Shootman, break through the artificial silos companies have traditionally structured around departments. How? By tying the efforts and decisions made throughout an organization to the one thing that truly matters: revenue. More precisely, sustained revenue growth.

Revenue Engine is the culmination of many years studying what tactics drive continued revenue performance at the fastest growing companies. Steven and Alex provide case studies, concepts and ideas that help you grow revenue. They explain why data is your best friend when it comes to eliminating choke points in your growth strategy. They show how to read buyers' digital behaviors to tailor your messaging. In the final chapter they bring all the ingredients to a boil in accessible, but comprehensive language.

The result is a primer for how to implement best practices and tips proven to increase revenue. But Steven and

Alex go even further, eliminating the psychological barriers that too often block organizations from succeeding in a fast-moving marketplace. It is a handbook not only for how businesses with global aspirations should function today but for how they will operate tomorrow.

The new tools available to companies and consumers don't change the key element of any sales and marketing process. Buying and selling has always been about initiating a conversation. Conversion is about building those conversations into relationships.

Buyers' ability to educate themselves means an elevated conversation. Read this book and you'll be a welcome presence at the dinner party.

Brian Fetherstonhaugh
Chairman + CEO
OgilvyOne Worldwide

ACKNOWLEDGEMENTS

The process of writing a book is one that involves extraordinary efforts on the part of so many people. We owe a debt of gratitude to everyone who assisted us in the process of creating *Revenue Engine*, through ideas, encouragement, guidance, editing, reviewing, critiquing, and assistance. While it's impossible to thank everyone involved, we'd like to extend our thanks to a few folks who made this project possible through their contributions.

Jocelyn Brown, Paul Teshima, and Lori Niles-Hofmann, thank you for extremely detailed reviews of the content, challenging ideas, and guiding the overall structure of the book. Without your efforts, the book would not be what it is today. A heartfelt thanks to the Eloqua services team, who tackles the challenge of building revenue engines for their clients every day. Adrian Chang, Chad Horenfeldt, Nadia de Villa, Sarita Givens, Andrew Stafford, Jason Pemberton, Heather Foeh, Tim Hester, and Jen Rodrigues, thank you for the conversations, client stories, anecdotes, ideas, and metrics, that guided the book and added much needed color and depth.

Every client we've had the pleasure of working with has contributed to the insights upon which this book is based, and we both thank each of you deeply for the honor of working with you as you tackle the revenue engine challenges specific to your business. Chris Boorman, Mark McCary, Dianne Hardin, Rita Selvaggi, and Shanel Vandergriff, thank you for allowing your stories to be shared with a wider audience and anchoring many of the concepts throughout the book in your experiences.

Jen Horton, Laura Cross, Rhonda Wunderlin, thank you for your guidance and insights into the metrics that are most effective across such a broad range of marketers and vertical. Jackie Kiley and Lorna Nightingale, thank you for sharing your experience in driving those metrics to the level of depth that you are able to with your deep experience. Jim Williams, Elle Woulfe, Amber Stevens, Alex Fisher, Erika Goldwater, and the great folks on the Eloqua marketing team, thank you for challenging our thinking on naming, branding, and conveying key concepts. Joe Chernov, Jesse Noyes, thanks for pushing the boundaries of our thinking on the role of social media within an organization.

The great roster of sales executives who kept us focused on making the number when we leaned into the theoretical; Tom Schodorf, Andy Langsam, Steve Rowland, Craig Harper, Scott Schoonover, Kathy Bexley and Darroll Buytenhuys (aka 'Coach').

David Meerman Scott and Brian Fetherstonhaugh, thank you for advice throughout the process on books, branding, selling, and marketing. You've given so many great pearls of wisdom it would be hard to name them all, but your guidance has been greatly appreciated. Greg Alexander, your insights on the true cost of sales have been critical to unlocking the economics of the *Revenue Engine*. Art Wilson and Mike Morten you two really stamped "it is all about the pipeline stupid" on our foreheads. Chelsea Moriarty and Chris Harmon, thanks for patient reviews, changes, and more reviews of cover art. Warren Huska, thanks for even more patiently working through so many revisions of all the internal artwork in the book.

Andrea Corey and Egan Cheung, thank you for bringing your deep insights into data and analytics to the project. Stuart Wheldon, and Greg Lui, thank you for continually challenging any assumptions or assertions that had too much of a North American bias. Jill Rowley and Melissa Madian, thank you for passionately representing the sales perspective in any discussions that leaned too far towards a marketing-centric view. Chris Petko, thanks for allowing us to dig into every metric you created in order to understand them from every direction.

Michael Dowding, Dave Morris, and Val Sherer, thank you for your patience with the overall project, and for keeping us on track throughout the writing, editing, layout, and final efforts to get the book to print.

Joe Payne and Brian Kardon, thank you for encouraging us to tackle the book project and tell the story of the marketers who are changing the face of revenue generation. Without your unwavering support (and occasional prodding) it would not have happened.

Last, but far from least, we'd each like to thank our families for everything they do on a daily basis that makes everything that we do possible at all. Amita, Sejal, thank you for the encouragement and support throughout the entire book-writing process, and through the travel, both past and future, that the book entails. Will and Sam, thanks for not calling me Uncle Dad when I come home after many days on the road and Brettne thanks for the love and support you have always provided over the last 27 years.

With our deepest gratitude and appreciation,

Steve and Alex

CONTENTS

Part 2
Stop Crunching Numbers —Start Crushing Them . . 129

Chapter 7 See: Sunlight is the Best Disinfectant 131

PART

REVENUE PERFORMANCE MANAGEMENT

ONE

IT'S (NOW) ALL ABOUT REVENUE GROWTH

THE NEED FOR REVENUE PERFORMANCE MANAGEMENT

In the last century and a half, wave after wave of new ideas, new technologies, new visions, and new leaders have emerged to transform the way our society transacts business. These waves of innovation have brought with them new levels of efficiency, visibility, and control—and that's led to a new generation of leaders who are comfortable with upending the status quo.

Perhaps the most widely discussed transformation—and with one of the greatest impacts—was the advent of

Frederick Taylor's *scientific management* in the late 1800s and early 1900s. Best exemplified by Henry Ford in the production of the Model T, scientific management is an approach that analyzes and synthesizes workflows to optimize productivity. By breaking down an operation into a series of repetitive tasks and then optimizing each task, scientific management gave rise to the phenomenon of mass production—the manufacture of a large volume of consistent product. By continuing to refine and optimize a process, manufacturers could continually reduce their costs and sell their goods for significantly lower prices.

The second major business transformation: the adoption of *total quality management* (TQM), advocated by W. Edwards Deming in the 1940s and 1950s. Through a relentless focus on statistical methods to reduce process deviances and improve overall quality, TQM enabled companies to consistently produce higher quality products at lower cost. Organizations like Toyota leveraged these techniques with great success to leapfrog entrenched competitors and assume industry leadership.

Similarly, *supply chain management* has evolved from its roots in the 1960s, enabled by the first *electronic data interchange* (EDI) systems. In the 1990s, *enterprise resource planning* (ERP) software and radio frequency ID (RFID) tags emerged as important business innovations. Each of these business evolutions transformed an area of significant corporate expenditure and enabled early adopters to establish an unassailable lead. In fact, a strategic focus on SCM enabled Walmart to dominate the discount retail sector in North America.

As the 20th century drew to a close, business-process reengineering presented an equally transformative perspective on the business processes within an organization. Concurrently, the stage-gate methodology was being applied to research and development to systematize and optimize the launch of new products.

THE FINAL FRONTIER FOR TRANSFORMATIVE INVESTMENT

The common thread among each of these revolutionary transformations? They targeted major, specific sources of corporate *expenditures*. Scientific management optimized gross margins by minimizing manufacturing costs. Supply chain management reduced COGS by optimizing inventories and lowering supplier costs. Business process reengineering reexamined all areas of a business process and challenged the necessity of many G&A functions, while the

Figure 1.1 – Share of Net Revenue

Share of Net Revenue	Median
Net Revenue	100.00%
Total Cost of Goods Sold	26.88
Gross Margin	62.50
Research and Development	28.95
Sales & Marketing	39.78
General & Administrative	29.31
Total Operating Expenses	97.23
Operating Income (Loss)	
Other Income (Expense)	

? Control & Optimization

stage-gate methodology ensured that R&D investments were properly allocated.

Conspicuously absent from this relentless focus on improvements: investments in *revenue*. The "cost of revenue," expressed as a percentage of revenue, ranges from around 12 percent in industries such as financial services to nearly 40 percent in the software industry. As paradoxical as it sounds, the discipline of earning revenue represents a significant area of expense. That's why companies need to dramatically improve their level of control and to optimize the processes they use to attract and secure revenue –on a par with the attention other business disciplines have received over the past 150 years.

ENABLING THE TRANSITION

Each major transition has happened because of corresponding changes that took place in society and technology. If it wasn't for the early stages of mechanization that the Industrial Revolution ushered in (combined with the stopwatch and clipboard), the discipline of scientific management would likely have not taken place. A suite of technologies from the connected networks that enabled EDI to the innovations in RFID tagging enabled supply chain management to begin and thrive as a discipline. Similarly, statistical analysis tools and techniques provided the basis for the TQM discipline.

Marketing and Sales are Finally in Focus

Historically, marketing and sales have not been held to the same standards of measurement, optimization, and control that other corporate disciplines have confronted. Why? In a word: *visibility*. Scientific management was enabled by the ability to observe a worker, measure and time the tasks performed, and refine them accordingly. The tracking innovations in logistics and warehousing meant that analysts could track each package, each movement, and each shipment to a granular level, which gave rise to supply chain management. And the ability to precisely and automatically measure defect rates and manufacturing tolerances meant businesses could feasibly embrace and implement the total quality management discipline.

Unfortunately, that hasn't typically been the case with marketing initiatives or sales conversations that have long eluded meaningful measurement. Without the ability to see and measure the progress of buyers, it has been virtually impossible to systemically optimize the performance of the revenue creation process. Until now.

Unprecedented transitions in buyer behavior and online access to information over the past 10 years have enabled, for the first time, the management and optimization of the entire revenue-creation process.

Understanding Buyers

Thanks to sweeping adoption of increasingly sophisticated communication technology, today's leaders—who have the *responsibility* of driving the revenue engines of their business—also have the *luxury* of understanding more about individual buyer interests than ever before. While demographic or firmographic criteria may have been sufficient when broad, outbound messages were the mainstay of marketing, they are no longer remotely effective or sufficient in today's world.

Data is the non-negotiable foundation of buyer insight—it's the "table stakes" for serious marketing. But data alone isn't enough. It must also be extended and complemented by deep insights into buyer behavior, interests, and objections. To be of maximum value, these insights must be distilled into assessments of the roles each buyer plays, and where each buyer is in his or her unique buying process.

By understanding where each buyer is in the buying process, companies carefully allocate their marketing and sales resources to the stages of the buying process where they can have the most revenue impact. Detecting and decoding these "hints of intention" shows us a holistic picture of the buyer's role, interests, and propensity to buy that is equally valuable as, if not more valuable than, the insights a salesperson could gain from observing a buyer's body language in face-to-face interactions.

Digital Body Language

Savvy sales professionals know: in those crucial face-to-face interactions, each facial expression or body posture gives us a clue as to the individual's true motivations, interests, and opinions. Smiling, nodding, or leaning forward show interest and excitement. Frowns and furrowed brows express concern or hesitation. Crossed arms or a pushed-back chair indicate latent (perhaps overt) objections and potential disagreements.

Many early-stage sales engagements happen almost exclusively online today. Buyers don't meet a sales rep until they're much further along in their discovery process. They are researching purchase alternatives in-depth on websites. These buyers are receiving and forwarding e-mails. Fortunately, those online behaviors can give careful observers important clues regarding the buyer's interests, opinions, and motivations. Each Web page visited carries an indication of interest. Each e-mail that is opened or clicked indicates a response to a certain message. Each search phrase that is used to find information that has been shared displays hidden questions, objections, or interests on behalf of the prospect. Each visit to, or referral from, a social media discussion shows an area of interest and engagement. Collectively, this "digital body language" can be aggregated, sorted, and analyzed to derive a wealth of information about a prospective buyer.

A buyer's area of interest can be discovered and prioritized, her stage in the buying process can be pinpointed, and her objections can be anticipated and pre-handled. This digital body language provides the insights marketers need to deliver the right message to the right person at the right time. It can also show when the buyer is ready engage more fully in a sales process, or how a marketing campaign has performed in guiding prospects through the stages of their individual buying processes.

Deep Insights, Profound Opportunity

This deep, granular set of insights into buyer actions, interests, and intentions provides the largest opportunity ever seen to enhance the revenue-focused disciplines of marketing and sales. Much as stopwatches, statistics packages, and RFID unleashed fundamental transformations of manufacturing, quality control, and logistics, the ability to understand each indication of buyer interest and intent can fundamentally reshape the art and science of generating revenue.

NEW REALITIES OF GROWING REVENUE

But this opportunity also brings a challenge. The same forces that enable stronger revenue performance can dramatically change the role of marketing and sales in profound ways. After all, at their heart, marketing and sales are information-conveying disciplines. We must carefully select and frame every aspect of the information we present to buyers. From mass communication channels to one-on-one conversations, marketers and salespeople must skillfully guide and channel the buyer's attention, interests, behaviors, and motivations. Through this guidance, they move buyers from a state of minimal awareness and interest to one where they are actively interested and motivated to make an appropriate purchase decision.

While purchasing is an information-intensive process, forward-thinking marketing and sales professionals recognize that they are no longer the exclusive providers of that information. The information available online continues to expand at ever-increasing rates. This includes information from third parties that often carries higher levels of credibility with buyers. As this happens, we must rethink how we use marketing and sales to guide buyers toward favorable purchase decisions.

The Changing Buyer

In the last few years, buyer efficiency has accelerated. This trend has been with us since the first days of the Internet, but now, buyers can quickly, efficiently, and freely access almost any information they need to learn about new market spaces, educate themselves on what is possible, form opinions on how it might work within their own business, and whittle down lists of vendors to help them with the challenge.

This frankly radical change in buyer access to information continues to accelerate with each new information-sharing platform, social network, and technology innovation that achieves broad adoption. For example, even two years ago, it would have been difficult to envision how smartphones are changing the retail experience. Now, buyers standing in the aisles at crowded malls are taking out their phones, quickly scanning independent reviews and buyer comments before making purchase decisions. They are also using these same smart phones to instantly access online coupons that are dynamically presented based on their history as a consumer. As phenomena like these take hold, marketers and salespeople who fail to adapt will continue to find themselves disintermediated and struggling to achieve results that are even on par with what they achieved in previous years.

An Evolving Buying Process

For all those who understand the implications and embrace this exciting change, there is an unprecedented opportunity to fundamentally rethink and reinvent what it means to market and sell. Yesterday's model of merely pushing undifferentiated messages and products on a mass audience no longer works. Today, marketers and salespeople are zeroing in on how buyers proceed through a sales process, what stages they go through, and what perception shifts and learnings take place along the way. When we understand these crucial milestones, we can tailor the information we provide so that it responds precisely to each buyer's unique needs.

With this knowledge, innovative marketers and salespeople can implement creative ways to guide buyers along a structured process. Careful selection of topics, timings, and information-delivery channels allow buyers to engage in a process of self-directed, self-paced discovery—instead of enduring increasingly ineffective broadcast and interruption-based techniques.

Explosion of Communication Platforms

Anyone involved in marketing over the last few years has seen the rapid proliferation of communication, messaging, and interaction platforms. We're seeing new ways for audiences to engage with one another and with the many independent third-party organizations in their industry—and it's futile to even attempt to keep on top of every one of these communication platforms. Nonetheless, marketing and sales leaders must properly assess and understand which forums and channels are worthy of investment in, either to connect with prospective buyers or guide the perspectives of key influencers.

To assess which communication platforms are relevant, we first need a framework to understand how communication within today's environment helps guide each individual buyer through his journey of education and discovery.

Most critically, however, each new communication platform offers a new level of insight into buyer behavior and response that was simply unavailable in the mass communication platforms of yesterday. Each click, view, tweet, and "like" indicates what an individual buyer has found interesting.

Collectively, these trends guide us toward a profound rethinking of how we build, staff, motivate, and measure the groups within our organizations who drive revenue. Buyers are now armed with information sources that are many times deeper than what was available even a decade ago. As a result, they will demand significantly different interactions than buyers who lack these rich insights. Marketers face a bewildering array of new communication forums and vehicles and now must wisely choose where and how to allocate their scarce resources. Sales professionals, confronting highly informed buyers, must adapt their selling efforts to guide these buyers rather than assume they hold knowledge the prospect requires. Salespeople are no longer the gatekeepers.

At the same time, executives leading these organizations must provide the guidance, frameworks, and analyses to show where efforts must be focused, what works, and what doesn't. Only then can we begin to manage the overall performance of revenue generation and achieve *revenue performance management* excellence.

THE REVENUE ENGINE

This book is a guide for executives seeking to make sense of, tap into, and capitalize on the changes in buying behavior today. By revisiting how revenue is generated within a business from the perspective of the buyer, we have an opportunity to build a revenue engine that leverages today's tools, platforms, and communication approaches in ways that make revenue generation understandable, optimizable, and measurable.

To frame this discussion on building a new revenue engine, it helps to start with a definition.

The Definition of a Revenue Engine

The revenue engine of a company is the overall system by which buyers are made aware of a company's products or services, guided through an education period in which they form opinions and preferences, brought together with sales professionals at a time of mutual benefit if necessary, and ultimately helped to make a positive buying decision. Crossing the disciplines of both marketing and sales, the revenue engine is co-managed by both groups.

Figure 1.2

Revenue performance management must be built on a backbone that encompasses a number of complementary technologies and supporting processes to accomplish the following five elements of revenue performance management:

> The revenue engine of a company is the overall system by which buyers are made aware of a company's products or services, guided through an education period in which they form opinions and preferences, brought together with sales professionals at a time of mutual benefit if necessary, and ultimately helped to make a positive buying decision.

1. **Discoverable Information**

   Marketers engaging with new-breed buyers need ways to make the information their buyers need "discoverable" by those buyers. Whether actively

sought, or passively stumbled upon, this information must be there at the right moment, and in the
right media channel to catch the buyer's attention.

2. **Buyer Stage Understanding**
   Today's best sales and marketing professionals focus
   on understanding where each buyer is in his or her
   unique buying process. This understanding is derived by analyzing all available data about the buyer,
   especially through careful observation of their
   online behavior and digital body language.

3. **Coordinated Efforts**
   Instead of acting independently on unrelated efforts, sales and marketing teams must collaborate
   to optimize the allocation of resources in a way that
   maximizes and accelerates the way buyers move
   toward the desired purchase decision.

4. **Clean Data**
   Like clean oil for a high-performing engine, clean
   data is crucial for optimal revenue performance
   management. High-performing revenue processes
   ensure the consistency, completeness, and quality of
   the underlying data at all points in the process.

5. **Actionable Analysis**
   For executives responsible for growing revenue in a
   business, analysis is only valuable if it drives *action*.
   Likewise, revenue performance can only be managed if you correctly allocate investments and properly analyze their resulting effects.

Marketing and sales leaders who build effective and efficient revenue engines will see their strategic relevance increase as they increasingly anticipate, forecast, and guide revenue many months or quarters in advance— with greater precision. Conversely, those who fail this test will see significant and steady erosion in both their ability to precisely pair marketing and sales investments with the right challenges in the buying process, and their strategic relevance at the executive table.

TWO

SEARCH IS THE NEW SALESPERSON

MAKE INFORMATION DISCOVERABLE

As legendary management guru Peter Drucker reminds us, the goal of any business is simple: to create and keep customers. Unfortunately, for many businesses, creating a customer often involves a lengthy—sometimes torturous—process that a customer must endure. He must be educated. Perceptions must change. Objections must be overcome. And decisions must be coordinated.

That's where marketing traditionally comes in. Marketing and sales provide the information—in widely varying forms—to the prospective buyers that educates, persuades, and encourages them to reach the desired decision outcome. However, the fundamental shift in how buyers access information is rewriting many of the conventional rules for marketing and sales.

Figure 2.1

THE NEW WAYS BUYERS ACCESS INFORMATION

Today, a relentless onslaught of innovative technologies, behavior patterns, and approaches are changing the marketing and sales environment. Given this, it can be difficult to discern what the significant underlying trends are. Today, marketers are tracking rapid changes in social media and search marketing, and the decreasing relevance of print and mass media. The underlying trend driving this, however, is simply access to information. To properly understand this in context, we need to reach back in history several hundred years. Today's information trends, in fact, start all the way back with Johannes Gutenberg's invention of movable type in the 15th century.

With the invention of the Gutenberg press, mankind achieved, for the first time, the ability to mass-produce and distribute information at exceptionally lower costs and higher speeds. This revolutionary access to information caused profound shifts in society, including advances in science and philosophy that ultimately led to the Renaissance.

Quality, Filters, and Economics

This unprecedented access to information was quickly harnessed through fairly basic economics. The fixed cost to set up a new book for a print run, and the marginal cost to print individual books were incurred upfront. The revenue from selling those books was realized after they were sold—after printing. This simple structure, shared by all forms of mass media—television, radio, movies, music, newspapers—created the driving dynamic of mass media. The publisher, as the one who made the upfront investment, was forced to act as a quality filter on the information being published simply by the economics of the situation.

If a publisher properly selected content that interested large audiences, he sold a large number of books (or, of course, more recently, CDs or movies) for minimal incremental cost, and earned a significant profit. Conversely, if a publisher did not act appropriately as a quality filter, he would create products not purchased by the audience, preventing the recoup of his upfront investments and quickly leading to bankruptcy.

Over time, this meant that markets built a level of trust in the quality and consistency of the content that could be expected from each publishing source. Today, leading media sources like *The Wall Street Journal, Harvard*

Business Press, CNN, and Fox News are expected by their audiences to produce content of a particular style and quality. They do this because it is an economic imperative. Accordingly, audiences rely on their preferred publishers to act, essentially, as filters for the information they consume.

The Mass Audience and Mass Marketing

Since larger audiences deliver increasingly sound economics, the media began to thrive. As they did, they offered marketers highly compelling opportunities. For a fee, the publisher would allow the marketer to bypass the filter of quality (within reason, of course) to deliver a message to its audience. This was referred to as a "media buy" where one placed an "advertisement." But from an information-flow perspective, marketers paid publishers fees to bypass the editorial filter on information quality. Through this arrangement, publishers had to maintain an appropriate balance between the amount of advertisements and the quality of their editorial content to maintain the audience's attention and, of course, purchases.

This straightforward framework quickly became the dominant marketing and advertising paradigm from the 1940s to the early part of the first decade of the new millennium. Many variations of the basic model emerged in which the three basic parameters of the system were adjusted:

- The percentage of revenue generated from readers *vs.* from advertisers

- The medium through which the information was published
- The style in which the advertisement was presented

Regardless of the fine-tuned nuances, this same basic model remained intact for decades. Even the first decade of Internet marketing largely followed this model.

Marketing in a Mass Media World

Within this environment of mass-outbound messaging to an audience developed by publishers, the modern discipline of marketing developed. Frameworks such as Philip Kotler's well-studied "Four Ps" (product, price, place, and promotion) were used to structure messaging campaigns. These were simple, but effective, tools for planning marketing messages in environments where the audience was only defined by basic demographics and firmographics (who the people and businesses were), and by general shared interests, such as subscription to a particular magazine. Adding to their effectiveness was the fact that marketers were, at that time, the main sources of information on a company's products and services, and therefore played a key role in the buyers' education process.

Communication with a mass audience, without knowing whether that audience is actively interested in making a purchase, meant marketers could use only the broadest, or "lowest common denominator" messages. Audience breadth and the lack of insight into individual buyer interests and needs meant marketers continually shifted their messaging away from specifics and toward higher-level, broader-value themes.

This meant that marketing almost exclusively delivered branding and high-level awareness. But there was no way to pinpoint the key buyers who were beginning to move toward the investigation or validation stages of the buying process. This small subset of the audience, that was actively engaged in buying activity, was not cost-feasible to target directly through mass media tools, so the information they required was not made available to them through marketing.

The result: interested, motivated buyers who needed specific information on capabilities and fit for a particular business situation needed to interact directly with a salesperson to acquire that information.

Sales in a Mass Media World

In parallel with marketing's efforts to achieve high-level awareness and branding, the discipline of sales evolved to work with individual prospective buyers. Successful sales processes aligned around common structures. Most frameworks began with a conversation commonly referred to as the "discovery call" where the salesperson learned about the prospective buyer's needs, and, in exchange, educated the buyer with a basic overview of the product or service being offered.

Over time, as the salesperson guided and educated his prospect, he learned more about her business challenges. As a key conduit of information about his industry and products/services, and how they might best be deployed in the prospect's business environment, he was needed for this education process. Skilled salespeople used this access to develop the deep relationships and trust needed to guide a prospect to a favorable decision.

The Sales and Marketing Divide

This difference in roles, based on information flow, led to a structural divide between marketing and sales. Marketing would communicate high-level messages, while sales worked with individual prospects. This divide led to a gap between the two departments that is still present—and still creating challenges—today. Historically, marketing has lacked the processes, experience, and tools to sufficiently understand the buying intentions of individual prospects. Sales has been oriented around providing very specific knowledge to prospective buyers, one organization at a time, and has not historically thought in terms of broader communication options or understanding buyer interests prior to that initial conversation.

This difference in capabilities led to a significant divide between the two organizations. The skills, metrics, and approaches differed so significantly between the mass communications of the marketing department and the individual conversations in sales that the two groups became fundamentally separate. Having two separate departments became the norm in most organizations.

At the same time, because of the gap between the scope of operations of each group, there was no need for any significant coordination between the two. This divide, and the friction it creates, still exists in many organizations to this day, even though the fundamental reason for the gap's existence is no longer valid. Overcoming the sales and marketing divide is a necessary step in creating an efficient revenue engine.

CHANGING ECONOMICS, CHANGING INFORMATION ACCESS

Over the last decade, we've seen profound changes in the underlying economics of information access. Today, content owners can create content in any media type—text, audio, video—and make it available to every person on the planet at essentially zero incremental cost. This is a profoundly transformative capability that revolutionizes the dynamics between publishers and consumers. Whether it's a website, an e-book, a video, a podcast, or a blog post, the publisher incurs such a small cost in creating or distributing the content, that there is no obligation to apply a quality filter or ensure that the recipient pays an appropriate amount.

By eliminating incremental costs, we remove the economic quality filter that publishers were historically burdened with. As a result, an exponentially increasing universe of content is available. Within this universe of content, however, we no longer have the same techniques to filter the quality of information. There is no economic reason for the content to be of a minimum level of quality as determined by its interest to an audience—because *there is no economic requirement to have an audience in order to publish content.*

Fortunately, the market has stepped into this void, with a variety of new and innovative ways to filter information for quality. All of them are inherently social.

Search: The Original Social Filter

The concept of social filtering is very simple: a piece of content is good if other people like it. At their core, today's search engines are inherently social. Content receives a high rank if other people like it as evidenced by them linking to it from another Web page. Although it's a simple construct, the use of links to define popularity and rankings has become immensely powerful. Traditionally, it was the major publishing houses and editorial groups of newspapers and television stations who determined what information was presented. Today, those gatekeepers have been replaced. The filtering by major search engines is arguably a much greater factor in determining what information gets presented to an audience.

Although most search engines allow targeted advertisements to be purchased alongside natural (sometimes called "organic") rankings, no major search engine allows a marketer to purchase a natural ranking position. Instead, the high ranking in a social filtering system must be earned by creating high-quality content and having it deemed as such by industry peers.

Social Filters: "You Might Like ..."

Social filters are rapidly moving ahead through a variety of social media sites such as StumbleUpon, Facebook "Likes," Reddit, and many more. These sites provide powerful ways for users to categorize, rank, and recommend interesting and relevant content for particular topics. Similarly, for both information and products, the history, experiences, and recommendations of other users are an increasingly common indicator of relevance and quality. For example, collaborative filtering techniques, popularized by Amazon's book recommendation engine, look at the interaction history of thousands of other people to determine, based on their decisions and your similarity to their prior history, which product or content is most likely to interest you.

The major search engines continue to improve and refine their algorithms. As they do, they are giving greater emphasis to the social use and recommendation of content. Today, search engines are also looking at how often content is shared, posted, Liked, or Tweeted, as they revamp their algorithms to rank search results and improve their accuracy and relevance.

Social Influence Continues to Evolve

Increasingly, social media sites are providing new ways to list, rank, and categorize participants. Although implemented in different ways, the idea is universal: empower broad audiences to define who they are influenced by, by topic. The rationale is easy to understand in an off-line context: the person we turn to for advice on home-theater equipment might not be the same person we turn to for restaurant recommendations or the best travel deals. A person with interests in wine, cars, and restaurants, for example, will likely be influenced by different individuals in each topic.

High-level metrics of influence, such as the number of "friends" or "followers," or even message-forwarding likelihood, are too basic. They lack the idea of context, which is critical for understanding influence. Just because a person is widely followed for his opinions on cars, doesn't mean we should grant him any credibility when he shares an opinion on wine.

This challenge is being tackled, however, by a few key innovative solutions. By looking at a variety of factors such as the "lists" a person appears in, the topics they talk about, and which of those topics appear to influence their social network, a person's influence can be broken down into topic categories.

This influence segregation becomes vital when we use social criteria to govern search results. A wine-related link that is shared by 10 wine experts should receive a much higher social ranking than a link that is shared by 100 people who do not have a social profile showing they are respected by their peers on wine-related topics.

The credibility and authority we granted to the major publishers based on their overall audience size is now being parceled out to an infinitely broader, granular, and finely tuned audience. Previously, an advertisement in a major topical/trade publication may have been the best way to reach an audience. Now, that access is through social media. If the key influencers in your topic area see content or viewpoints as relevant and correct, it will become discoverable to those who are interested in that topic area within a much broader network.

Information Will Find Me

The logical extension of social influence on information discovery is that information consumers—our prospective buyers—will begin to expect that the information they want will "find them." Just as songs, books, and movies are recommended to us in the consumer world based on collaborative filtering techniques, information in the business world may soon find us as well.

A combination of our own unique social graph, and that social graph's interests and reading history, could soon transform information discovery from active discovery into a passive recommendation. As each individual's interests, business role, and social influence graph become increasingly known to search engines and content

Case Example

Since their founding, SolarWinds believed in providing access to a wealth of information of relevance to buyers. Selling initially into the community of network engineers and architects, they realized that their buyers very frequently searched for the solutions to specific technical problems. This technical audience was also the purchase decision-makers in most cases, so SolarWinds invested in content that addressed a wide variety of specific technical problems that a network engineer might be looking to solve. This long tail of highly technical content was discovered by buyers at the exact moment when they had a specific technical problem, and were most likely to be interested in the solution SolarWinds offers.

portals, the information they present will align more tightly with the person's interests.

Analytics across extremely broad populations and vast amounts of data on what consumers actually click or view will enable this selection and presentation to become startlingly precise, further increasing its effectiveness, adoption, and relevance to marketers.

Deeper Searches

Even for information being actively sought/pursued by potential buyers, significant changes are afoot. Buyers are rapidly becoming accustomed to the availability of vast amounts of valuable information online. And the increasing accuracy of search engines (using social influences to guide results), is leading searchers to adapt how they perform specific searches.

For instance, rather than search for broad topic areas (akin to flipping to a section of a newspaper), prospective buyers are using longer search terms to pinpoint the exact information they want. A number of studies have shown that the majority of search phrases being used today involve more than three words with many five words or longer. This is a significant development because it means prospective buyers are no longer seeking high-level topical information on general categories. Instead, they are targeting much deeper information that fits a very specific challenge or precise question.

As they stay aware of the happenings in an area of their industry, buyers may also search for how specific new capabilities affect their industry (*i.e.* "augmented reality in real estate") or trends in businesses like theirs (*i.e.* "small-business adoption of CRM"). As they move toward a purchase cycle and look for vendors to evaluate, prospective buyers may seek particular traits (*i.e.* "funds making ethical investments in Latin America") or specialized capabilities (*i.e.* "high availability network backup solutions").

Similarly, when moving toward the final stages of a purchase decision, the searches made by prospective buyers may involve specific brands or product names, along with capabilities, objections, or perspectives of previous buyers (*i.e.* "Eloqua e-mail deliverability specifications" or "Eloqua marketing automation in financial services").

The resulting challenge for marketers is interesting. If searches become more precise, we must strive to create a wealth of interesting, relevant content at all phases of the buying process. Similarly, as search results are increasingly guided by social influence, we must also build influence and reputation among the appropriate audiences so that our results are found to be relevant.

ENGAGING THE CHANGED BUYER

These transformations in how buyers access information are the most profound changes we have seen since the advent of mass media. Marketers and salespeople seek to influence the likelihood that buyers will discover and select their products through the careful use of information. Therefore, this change in buyer behavior means that marketing and sales must also undergo a most fundamental change.

Marketers can no longer sit back and "buy attention" through mass media and then rely on professional salespeople to step in to guide buyers from discovery call through close. We now must recognize that buyers are in near-total control of their own buying processes and the information those buying processes require. We can look to guide, influence, and facilitate those buying processes, but we can no longer force them to happen or create them.

Denying these trends is not a viable strategy. As buyers grow accustomed to seeking information sources that they expect to be freely available online, information will appear to fill any vacuum. If your organization does not contribute to the knowledge, insights, facts, and opinions being sought, your competitors will be happy to fill that breach.

To build an effective revenue process, today's best marketers must ensure that all information their buyers need throughout the entire buying process is readily available. Marketers must ensure this information is readily discoverable in all buying stages—from awareness through investigation and finally to validation. Success can only come by embracing this trend. This means engaging and guiding today's buyer in new ways that reflect the new realities of information access and that, in turn, rely on understanding each buyer.

Historically, we might have understood each buyer through face-to-face interactions, but now we typically only see the evidence of their online interactions. Luckily, this does not leave us blind, as each online interaction leaves a trace—a hint at their digital body language—that clues us into their interests and buying process.

THREE

THE MIND OF THE BUYER

UNDERSTANDING AND MODELING HOW BUYERS BUY

Revenue performance management is rooted first and foremost in clearly understanding buyers' interests, motivations, and goals from the earliest stages of awareness through to purchase, account growth, and advocacy of our solutions. Each marketing or sales initiative must facilitate one aspect of this buying process. But we can only do

Figure 3.1

so once we have fully and clearly obtained a thorough understanding of the entire buying continuum.

THE BUYING PROCESS

Buyers progress through a buying process at their own pace. They are motivated or triggered by internal events at their company, guided by conversations with peers, and influenced by chance discovery of information. While we are not privy to these internal events and conversations, we can see their effects on buyers by observing what each buyer does online and using that behavior to approximate what motivations or internal events might have caused those actions.

As marketers, we can, at best, ensure that the best possible content for inspiring action, changing mindsets, spurring change, or overcoming objects is in place, and likely to be discovered by the appropriate prospect. We cannot force the action to happen or the mindsets to change. However, by understanding the historical trends on the likelihood of a buyer at one phase of the buying process to move to the

Figure 3.2 **The Buying Process**

next, and the time it typically takes for this transition to happen, we can begin to model the buying process in a surprisingly accurate way.

Case Example

FifthThird bank found an indication of the length of time involved in their buyers buying process through analyzing the results of a marketing campaign that they did in February of 2010. The marketing campaign was a simple series of three emails with information on a new resource center they had deployed with information on their new Check Image Processing Network. The email was sent to 3500 prospective customers at various stages of their buying cycle, including some who were in new territories for FifthThird, and likely quite unfamiliar with their offerings. The initial response was typical; a reasonable amount of engagement from those who were already interested in FifthThird, and almost no response from the very early stage prospects.

However, by sending their sales team notifications whenever qualified buyers visited the resource center, they noticed an interesting secondary effect. Many of the early stage prospects had kept the email as a reference sheet, and could still be seen referring back to it as late as October of that year, eight months later. While they were not actively investigating solutions in February, the awareness generated by the initial campaign slowly trickled into results as business needs brought those prospects forward into an investigation process many months later.

Stages of the Buying Process

Each organization, and in fact each product line within each organization, sees buyers progress through a buying process that is unique to that product. However, all buying processes can be loosely categorized into three main stages, each with its own challenges:

1. **Awareness and Education**

   In this very early stage, the potential buyer begins to learn what might be possible in this market space. A veteran might learn about new regulatory trends, technology capabilities, or service innovations that might enable something previously not possible. A "rookie" buyer who is new to his role might come up to speed on various options to invest in. At a certain point, the awareness and education combine with business or economic events and opportunities to compel the buyer to consider an investment to seize the business opportunity or alleviate the business pain.

   At this point, in all likelihood, the marketing team isn't even aware of the buyer. Much of the early-stage self-education takes place anonymously. Some of this education may take place on the corporate website or social media presence, and some may take place on websites that are beyond the corporate Web presence, such as on industry sites, community forums, social media discussions, and news/analysis sites.

2. Investigation

In this stage, the buyer investigates solutions more deeply to understand how they might fit within her business environment. She may assemble a list of potential vendors to investigate to uncover a solution that roughly achieves the desired goals. As the buyer progresses from awareness to investigation, she is likely still obtaining a significant amount of education on the solution category. However, now it is much more specific to vendor solutions and her exact business context.

As this phase proceeds, a team may begin to form (either officially or unofficially) to analyze the business challenge being considered. Soon, the team's consensus is reached on the need to make a purchase to solve the business challenge.

During this stage, the prospective buyer often becomes known to the marketing team as a result of some interaction or event attendance. However, the prospect is often "too early" in its own buying process to engage in a productive dialogue with sales. Until they conclude that a high-priority business problem can and should be addressed by the solution in question, it is likely that they will resist spending time with a sales organization.

3. Solution Validation

During the final stage of the buying process, the buying team reaches and justifies its decision. The capabilities of the specific solution under consideration are compared to the business challenge to ensure a good fit. Pricing and contract terms are negotiated, key stakeholders are engaged, and objections are overcome.

This final stage is where the vendor sales team is most heavily involved. The sales organization carefully orchestrates the deal and addresses all crucial decisions and stakeholders. Based on experiences shepherding similar deals, each sales team typically identifies a sequence of milestones to identify what key hurdles remain before a purchase is culminated.

Bear in mind, of course, that these stages are not purely sequential. Buyers do not often proceed through them in an orderly manner. Individual buyers often move back and forth, from stage to stage, as business conditions and needs continue to shift and evolve dynamically. For example, one buyer in the organization might only be learning about the capabilities available in the industry while her colleague is quite sophisticated in her understanding of the different vendor options. However, this rubric can serve as a useful model for thinking about the process as buyers progress through some form of each stage in all industries and organizations.

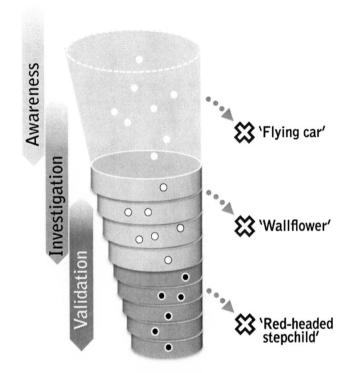

Figure 3.3 Leaks in the Buying Process

Leaks in the Buying Process

Each stage of the buying process presents its own challenges. Revenue teams must ensure that buyers don't stagnate at a particular stage and fail to continue. The three broad challenges, or "leaks" in the buying process, that organizations face are linked to the three general buying stages that buyers go through:

1. **The Flying Car**

    Your business can solve a problem that most of the world is unaware can be solved. Since they are unaware that a new solution exists, potential buyers blindly continue with their inefficient processes and methods and do not actively look for a solution.

2. **The Wallflower**

   The problem your business solves is known, but you are not a vendor that comes to mind when prospective buyers look for alternatives or seek new solutions for their specific business. You are never in the running.

3. **The Red-Headed Stepchild**

   The problem your business solves is known and you are evaluated when potential buyers look for solutions, but buyers rarely select your solution.

Clearly, these categorizations are very broad, but most marketing challenges loosely fall into one of these three categories. As each category refers to a way in which buyers leak from a buying process, focusing marketing and sales investments on plugging the leaks is the most critical thing for any organization to do. The first step, however, is arriving at a clear understanding of what the buying process looks like for the average buyer.

Mapping the Buying Process

Identifying, labeling, and mapping the stages of your unique sales cycle and buying process are more art than science in most cases. However, a strong framework can help you more clearly understand how your market buys and identify opportunities to further facilitate the buying processes.

In each stage of this framework, use one set of questions to examine and analyze whether there is a problem at all in that stage, a second set to understand how current buyers move through that stage, and a third set to assess where there are improvement opportunities for you in that stage. After performing this exercise, you will have a clearer view on where marketing and sales investments might be made to best help buyers arrive at a successful decision to purchase your solutions.

1. **Awareness and Education**
    a. **Is there a problem?**
        • Are prospective buyers generally aware of your solution category and what it can do for their business?

        • What are the opinions of industry analysts and what is their general knowledge of the market space and likely buyers?

        • What are your sales team's experiences with initial calls? Do prospects understand the business problem your solution solves?

        • What does firsthand survey research with likely buyers reveal?

    b. **What happens currently?**
        • How do existing prospects become educated about your category?

- Where do customers and prospects read about topics in your industry?
- What are the traffic sources for your educational or thought-leadership content?
- What do industry newsletters and sites tell you about current topics and do they include messages about your solution category?

c. **What are the options?**
- What ways could prospects potentially become aware of your category?
- What results get returned for searches on some terms related to pains that you solve (not terms that describe your category)?
- What events, tradeshows, and publications are well attended/read by key buyers in your industry?
- Which industry sites discuss you and/or your competitors frequently?
- Which websites are you currently seeing traffic from?

2. Investigation
  a. **Is there a problem?**
  - If prospects create a list of solution options, are you likely to be on that list?
  - Do you review competitor wins to understand whether you were considered?

- What percentage of the search phrases driving traffic to your site contain your brand or product names?

- How often are you added as a last-minute option in a purchase decision based on a cold call or chance encounter?

- What percentage of leads are originally sourced by marketing or arrive as inbound leads *vs.* those generated by a cold call?

b. What happens currently?
  - How have prospects typically found you?

  - What non-branded search terms drive traffic to your website?

  - How do inbound leads learn about you?

  - What's the breakdown of inquiries by source? In other words, what's driving early-stage inquiries?

  - What percentage of leads have been nurtured prior to becoming qualified leads?

c. What are the options?
  - How do prospective buyers build their list of potential vendors?

  - Which key industry comparison charts and analysts list solutions similar to yours?

  - Is your content featured in the results of search terms related to your category?

- What webcasts, videos, or talks from key industry influencers mention solutions like yours?

3. **Solution Validation**
   a. **Is there a problem?**
      - When a buyer evaluates your solution, do they select you?
      - What are your win/loss ratios for deals over the past few months or quarters?
      - What are your growth rates compared to competitors'?
      - Based on your loss-analysis, what are buyer reasons for choosing other vendors?
      - Are you ranked poorly in industry comparison charts?

   b. **What happens currently?**
      - How do buyers select a vendor?
      - How do competitors position your organization and your solutions?
      - What do third-party win/loss surveys reveal about buyer decision criteria?
      - Do the search phrases of website visitors that include your brand or product names also show objections or decision criteria?

- What do the marketing resources (whitepapers, case studies, free trials) actively used by buyers reveal about their current experience?

c. **What are the options?**
  - How can you better influence a buyer's decision process and criteria?
  - Who are the key analysts and influencers who guide the market?
  - How can you insert changes in buying criteria or positioning into your marketing messages to respond to changing buyer objections?
  - What are the common objections and do your current marketing assets address these objections?
  - Is your sales team connecting with the right prospects early enough to influence their buying decisions?

This is, of course, just a framework for thinking about the challenges. Every organization and industry deals with a different set of buying challenges. However, this framework can be quite useful for identifying gaps, challenges, or opportunities in the way your market currently buys.

SELLERS AND BUYERS

To move beyond the abstract, our understanding of how buyers buy must be viewed in terms of things that the marketer can see and understand. While much insight can be gained from the online behavioral cues and "footprints" that buyers leave, there is much that remains unknown. Similarly, while we can create relevant information at all stages of the buying process, we need to know a great deal about how buyers uncover information to ensure it is discovered at the right time by the right recipient.

Buyer Stage

As buyers move through their buying processes, the types and frequency of their activities provide savvy marketers with clues as to their buying stage. At the top of the funnel are the broadest universe of suspects who may be unaware of your solution category or, at least, not actively engaged in self-education.

Many individuals you engage with may keep themselves apprised of developments in your solution category on a casual basis, but are not engaged in an active buying process. Moving down the funnel, as buyers complete investigation and validation phases, their activity level picks up and the information they seek becomes more specific. There are usually significantly fewer individuals involved in these stages, which is why the funnel narrows toward the point at which a deal closes.

Marketing's role is to facilitate the larger number of prospects at early stages of the buying process, and move prospects from mildly interested to active buyers. Sales' role is to work with individual buying organizations to finalize a deal. As such, the funnel is a great representation of the two teams' overall challenge as the number of people being engaged shrinks toward the latter stages of the buying process. However, the funnel's implied linear progression is misleading. Realistically, most buyers move up and down the funnel in a very non-linear fashion.

For example, a prospect might move in and out of the funnel entirely over the course of months or years. Occasionally, he may show brief spurts of interest as he lightly self-educates on the industry, before falling back into inactivity. At certain points, a large amount of research and a significant amount of activity in a short time period may indicate the prospect has moved much further along in the buying process. But that can still be followed by a quiet period as internal business conditions lead to a temporary pause. This fluid dynamic leads to a perception of a "leaky funnel" because leads that seemed nearly ready for sales engagement almost inexplicably shift back to earlier phases of the buying process.

Overall, however, the funnel model does work as a useful construct. Generally, buyers progress through increasing levels of interest, and seek more precise topics of interest, as they move toward purchase. However, at an individual buyer level, the movement is much less linear. This means that marketers need to understand, at any point in time, where an individual lead is within the buying process.

What Can We Really See?

We've seen how prospects proceed through their own buying processes, but for revenue-focused executives to guide these buying processes, they must build an understanding of where each buyer is at any point in time. However, what marketers and sales executives can see is, of course, a highly imperfect, imprecise view. We can gather much data and assess where that buyer is, but the organization's view of its buying audience can only be an approximation of where each buyer is.

Looking at the buyer's world from the perspective of marketing, we can first categorize prospective buyers into four main categories:

- **Unknown:** We do not currently have a name, e-mail address, or other identifier for the person, but we may have seen her anonymous interaction with marketing assets on our website.

- **Known:** We have a valid and usable identifier such as an e-mail address, and can begin building an understanding of who this person is as a buyer.

- **Qualified:** Based on who the prospect is, and what she has done online she meets the definition of a marketing qualified lead, and we can engage the sales team to take the conversation further.

- **Closed:** All relevant questions and objections have been dealt with, and a deal has been signed.

Within these categories, there are a significant number of layers of understanding we must attain, but at a high level, the role of running the revenue engine for a business involves guiding buyers through these core stages.

Prior to Identification

In the early stages of awareness and education, a prospect is, in all likelihood, unknown to the seller. He may be learning about an industry or solution category by reading industry news sites or trade publications, or he might get industry knowledge from peers and influencers. Similarly, he may be encountering your advertising campaigns that target broad segments of buyers.

As this early stage, awareness building is now an increasingly an online activity, which gives us a greater ability to understand it as well. While it is not usually possible to identify specific individuals in these interactions, it's possible to understand audience sizes and rates of response. That gives a good sense of whether your current marketing investments are delivering a meaningful return.

Stages of Engagement

Once we've identified a buyer, we can assess how interested and engaged she might be. By analyzing the buyer's

Figure 3.4 - Sellers' View of Buyers

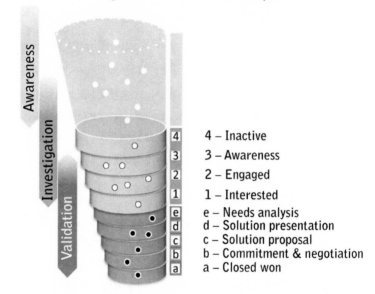

4 – Inactive

3 – Awareness

2 – Engaged

1 – Interested

e – Needs analysis
d – Solution presentation
c – Solution proposal
b – Commitment & negotiation
a – Closed won

"digital body language," we can apply rules to decode whether she is mainly interested in education and market awareness, has begun analyzing how your solution may fit her business, or has, in fact, attempted to validate the applicability of your solution to her needs.

Analyzing this digital body language to understand its meaning (in terms of buyer stage) is what the discipline of lead scoring focuses on. To understand buyer engagement, we categorize known buyers, prior to being qualified, based on their digital body language, into one of four levels:

4. **Inactive:** Either inactive or showing negligible interest in your company and its solutions within the last three months.

3. **Aware:** Some interest has been shown, but mainly in awareness and education-focused topics such as thought-leadership content and general education.

2. **Engaged:** A higher level of interest is shown, with a focus on specific topics, especially those that show how your solution might impact the buyer's specific business.

1. **Interested:** This is a more intense level of interest, with strong focus on the specifics of what an engagement might look like in terms of pricing, and objection-related topics.

These four levels of engagement must be defined in the context of your specific business, how your prospects reach a buying decision, and what level of insight their digital body language provides. However, this four-level style of framework provides a solid basis for understanding the engagement level of your prospects.

Sales Involvement

At a certain point, the buyer's interest profile is significant enough where it warrants the involvement of the sales team. This inflection point depends on many factors, including the buyer's willingness to engage with sales people, the competitiveness of the market, and the complexity of the solution(s) involved. Premature attempts to involve the sales team can lead to poor connection rates and frustrated buyers. Tardy attempts to involve sales can leave the door open to competitors to take greater control of the buying process and lead it in a direction that benefits them.

At this point, an opportunity is created and managed according to a defined sales process. While the buyer remains in control of much of the information he needs, the salesperson understands that, for a deal to happen, many hurdles must be overcome. For this reason, the stages in a sales process often reflect a combination of sales team tasks and milestones, such as gaining buy-in and sign-off from key stakeholders, as well as actions or expressions of interest from the buyer.

From the earliest point, when the prospect is unknown, through the period when buying interest is built and nurtured, and finally to the end of the process when a sale is consummated, the revenue team understands, at least approximately, where the buyer is in his buying process.

Discovery of Information

Understanding how buyers discover information is critical to identifying which revenue tools to apply. Whether it's an article title, an e-mail subject line, an outgoing direct-mail envelope, an interesting statistic, a tweet, a news headline, or a catchy name for an e-book, most of your potential market only encounters brief summaries of your content. Convincing your audience to take the next step—from headline to content—by clicking on (or otherwise engaging with) your content is as much art as it is science.

The art of writing provocative, catchy, and intriguing information summaries originally developed from newspaper headlines. The goal was to have the publication "discovered" by those passing by a newsstand. Now, in a world dominated by the need to make information discoverable, these skills are more critical than ever. Each article, headline, or tweet should be thought of in the same manner.

Now, this same idea of working to have prospective buyers "discover" information goes far beyond its roots in

Case Example

The sales team at FifthThird bank faced a challenge common to many well-established organizations. A tenured sales force, selling to established organization within a given territory, often had relationships with many of the prospects who fit the ideal profile of buyers. The challenge for them was then to understand exactly when to reach out to those buyers in order to spur a fruitful discussion. Calling too frequently would result in alienating the prospect, but missing an opportunity could mean losing out on millions of dollars of potential revenue. Timing was key. In order to optimize this process, the FifthThird sales team began to look for signs of engagement in order to prioritize their calls. When prospective buyers showed a spike in online activity, this was an indication that a business need might be present, and allowed for a well-timed call. Contrary to many calls without this insight, these calls were generally found to be very well received and often led directly to new business opportunities.

headlines, and is applicable in most of the media types we use today.

Discoverability: The Convergence of Mass Media and Direct Media

Historically, when we thought about marketing messages, we thought about two distinct categories of marketing efforts, at opposite ends of a spectrum. On one end, there's direct communication, where the individual's contact information is known and a message can be delivered directly. On the other end, we have mass media, where a broad audience is targeted based on demographics or audience characteristics.

This mental framework, however, obscures the fact that we truly have a spectrum. With recent advances in technology and transitions in buyers, we are seeing a trend from both ends of the spectrum toward the center.

Mass media, historically, was extremely broadly targeted, based on high-level demographics or audience profiles. It relied on the message being "discovered" by a small percentage of the viewing audience. With online media, the targeting of a message becomes increasingly

Figure 3.5 – **Discoverability**

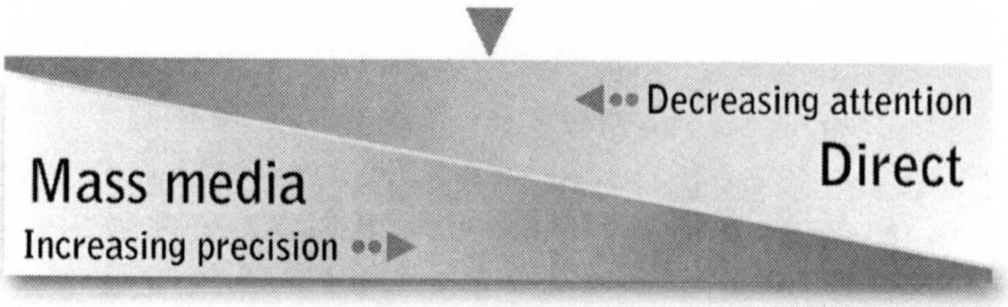

◀•• Decreasing attention

Mass media

Direct

Increasing precision ••▶

precise. Ads can be targeted based on behavior, demographics, or firmographics, almost down to the individual level. Search advertisements are targeted to the term being searched for. No longer are these purely mass audiences.

Similarly, with the exponential growth in all forms of direct communication, especially online forms such as e-mail, the challenge is no longer the delivery of the content—it's the *viewing* of the content. As e-mail inboxes get inundated with messages, Twitter streams fill with interesting links, and all forms of electronic communication zoom long past the point of saturation, the challenge is discovery. Great communicators who drive strong revenue performance for their organizations get their messages discovered by the recipient, even in a cluttered channel, rather than ignored or deleted.

GETTING INTO THE BUYER'S MIND: THE THREE MODES OF INFORMATION DISCOVERY

Prospects discover information through three main modes: passive discovery, active discovery, and influencer-based discovery. Revenue teams must understand each of these modes to enable their buying audiences to encounter the right information to guide their decisions.

Passive Discovery

Marketing has a long relationship with passive information discovery. Advertising and mass media are inherently passive-discovery techniques. Advertisements are placed in prominent locations (offline or online), and traffic arriving at the prominent location, usually driven by a related interest, encounters the messages.

However, passive discovery also extends into any situation where the prospect is not deliberately seeking the message being conveyed. Decreasing attention spans and increasingly precise targeting mean that even communication vehicles once thought of as exclusively direct can now be viewed as passively discoverable.

A prominent example: e-mail. While it can be directly delivered to an individual recipient, in no way does that guarantee it gets noticed or read. Virtually everyone receives more e-mail on a daily basis than we are able or willing to read. Typically a user scans through the inbox and makes very quick decisions on which messages to read and which to ignore or delete without reading. These snap judgments are typically based on the sender and the subject line. One or two uninteresting or non-valuable messages from a particular source will quickly lead the user to reflexively delete or ignore any future content. This is known as an "emotional unsubscribe"—the recipient has effectively tuned out of the communication without formally unsubscribing.

Typically, once an e-mail has been received and opened, the recipient quickly scans it for interesting content. If he discovers something that merits his time, he might read it. But if interesting content is not immediately

Case Example

Informatica found that their buyers discovered their solutions in two very distinct ways, and matched their effort in being discovered accordingly. The first way was around "broad topic problems" such as 'getting cost out of IT' or 'unlocking shareholder value in data'. For this type of problem, no direct solution was envisioned, and potential buyers were most interested in an intelligent discussion among peers and experts. This discussion might contain ideas of solutions that could be used, but it was mainly around approaches to consider. The second way was "narrow topic problems" such as 'Oracle application archiving' or 'master data management' where a direct solution was envisioned. In this case, potential buyers generally went directly to search in order to seek solutions for their business challenges. In each case, Informatica invested in being discovered based on exactly how buyers sought the information they needed.

apparent, the e-mail will be quickly deleted. This is why marketers must think of e-mail as a passively discoverable medium in the same way that we consider any topic shared in social media.

In all cases, the revenue team can increase the likelihood of engagement through creative advertising, catchy subject lines, or creative copywriting. However, the fundamental dynamic remains the same: *these are attempts to have a prospective buyer, who is not looking for information, discover something interesting about what is being offered.*

Active Discovery

With the growth of online information sources, it has become increasingly easier to quickly pinpoint information on almost any topic. Search is perhaps the most prevalent navigation paradigm, from Internet-wide searches on Google or Bing, and platform-specific searches such as Twitter or Facebook's internal search function, to topic-based alerts such as Meltwater or Google Alerts, and use-case-specific searches such as iPhone applications focused on movies or restaurants.

This active seeking of information gives marketers a unique opportunity to offer information to highly specific, tightly defined audiences of prospects—just by being found when information is sought. Search marketing, either natural or paid, is a great example of active discovery. A prospective buyer actively seeks information on a topic based on keywords. Successful marketers ensure their content is present at the top of the search results, either through an effective search engine optimization strategy, or good search engine marketing (and a healthy SEM budget).

While this definition of "audience" differs substantially from how we have used that term for outbound advertising, it is an equally relevant way to think about the information seekers. While an audience was historically defined as a group of people who received an outbound message, we can now think of them as the people, who, at any given moment, are seeking specific information. Delivering a message to this audience is equally, if not

Case Example

When addressing the "broad topic" questions around which buyers sought intelligent discussions rather than directly searching for topic information, the Informatica team worked to develop advocates, internal experts who could credibly join, start, and contribute to the ongoing discussions. The goal in this engagement was not to directly promote Informatica products, it was to build trust and credibility as an expert member of the community. As an advocate built trust and credibility within the community, they were able to carefully guide conversations, insert relevant facts and data, and introduce Informatica-related topics in a consultative, non-promotional way.

more, important than presenting a message to a passive audience through advertising.

Active searches for information also occur when prospects call a vendor organization, submit an online request for information, or attend a tradeshow seeking answers to specific questions. This information request is similar to a Google search in that it is a prospective buyer actively seeking information. Each way in which buyers actively seek information should be assessed to understand whether more resources should be assigned to optimize the efforts.

Influencer-Based Discovery

In both passive and active discovery, the goal is to get an idea, message, or piece of content to be discovered directly by an intended audience. This is, indeed, the main challenge of today's marketers. However, in most markets, there is also a core audience of influencers, advocates, and fans who can provide a third path through which information is discovered.

With the decline of mass publishers and the advent of online micropublishing (through industry sites, social media, communities, or discussion forums), marketers face a highly fragmented set of audiences. Each individual writer has unique motivations, such as building an audience and reputation, being viewed as an expert in a community, or developing a business.

By carefully building relationships with these influencers over time and understanding how you can help them achieve their goals, you can create a friendly crucible for each of your messages. Each of these individuals may have influence over an audience in a key market segment and collectively they may influence larger market areas than you could ever influence directly. Many key influencers in a particular space are also watched closely by the mainstream media.

By collaborating with this audience of influencers and advocates you can create a friendly launch pad and test site for any of your messages. Each story, and each message, must, of course, still stand on its own merits and be appropriately non-salesy. But an audience of advocates and fans, carefully nurtured, will give each message more open-minded consideration, and may be among the first to share it with their own audience.

In the various social media channels, information is not pushed out directly. Instead, it is published and discovered by an audience based on recommendations from peers, content syndication, and chance. The more interesting and relevant your content is, the more likely it is that your influencers will share it, forward it, and link to it, bringing it to the much broader audience that they influence—and that you want to reach.

Search giants are increasingly investing in technologies that map and model the social graph we are all a part of, making influencer-based information discovery even more robust and relevant. The next decade promises to be one where the mode of influencer-based discovery is equally, if not more, important than any other mode.

Unlike search marketing, however, there is no clear paid model for achieving broader distribution of your information within the social media world. Although a variety of economic structures are in development, none has achieved the wide acceptance we find with paid search marketing. This means that the most reliable way—indeed, perhaps the only way—to ensure your messages are fully discoverable in social media is to build strong relationships with the influencers in your space who are more likely to share those messages and ensure that your messages are sufficiently interesting, relevant, and non-salesy.

Your long-term reputation with each of these key influencers is based on a history of creating high-quality content. But each individual content piece stands on its own in terms of its inherent quality and sharability. The techniques of great journalists are instructive here in making each piece of content interesting and likely to be read.

FOUR

UNLOCKING THE BLACK BOX OF REVENUE INVESTMENTS

A FRAMEWORK FOR COORDINATING INVESTMENTS ACROSS MARKETING AND SALES

If buyers control their own buying process, it might be tempting to conclude that the disciplines of marketing and sales are waning. Of course, nothing could be further from the truth. The difference today is that marketing and sales no longer *control* the interaction. Instead, they must seek to influence buyers throughout their buying process, using the available tools, to optimally guide those prospective buyers toward a positive outcome.

With visibility into the buyer's progress in her unique buying process, an understanding of how likely she is to discover information, an awareness of which

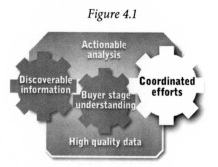

Figure 4.1

buyers are known and identified, and an assessment of the relative costs and value of each communication, we can begin to devise a comprehensive framework for allocating our marketing and sales investments.

If the top of the funnel is lighter than it should be, given revenue expectations and goals two fiscal quarters away, we can invest in initiatives that generate net new names, market awareness, and initial interest. If competitors are gaining market share in a particular segment and we learn that our organization is neither discovered nor invited to participate in sales situations, we might make an appropriate investment to improve our discoverability.

Similarly, if we find that win rates are dropping against certain competitors, we might invest in initiatives to educate influencers and buyers on the key purchase-decision criteria. By understanding the numbers, conversion rates, and timing of each stage of the buying process, we can seamlessly align marketing investments with the shortcomings of the revenue engine.

In making marketing investments, we must consider our buying audience—our target market. How do they discover information? Does our investment rely on knowing the individual? What are the relative costs and value of the communication vehicle?

INVESTING IN REVENUE

The revenue generation team has a wide array of tools and techniques at their disposal to provide information and guidance to prospective buyers, but must do so in a way that optimally engages the buyer. In analyzing where to make marketing or sales investments, view each investment in a comprehensive framework that allows the comparison of some very different investment types:

- **Buyer Stage**
  What stage of buyer interest does this type of investment typically cater to? Is this investment most appropriate for buyers at the Awareness, Investigation, or Validation stage of their buying process?

- **Information Discovery**
  How do we anticipate our buyers will discover the information we want to convey: Passive Discovery, Active Discovery, or Influencer-Based Discovery? Is it reasonable to expect they will discover information this way?

- **Known *vs*. Unknown Prospect**
  Does this communication rely on knowledge of the contact information for each individual? If so, are we confident we have the right and complete identifying information?

- **Paid *vs*. Earned Attention**
  In many investments, attention is acquired by allocating budget. However, in other marketing investments, attention is earned through direct engagement and content creation.

With this framework, and with an understanding of the buyer's journey, we can begin to understand the plethora of marketing and sales options available to us and think about tradeoffs not just within the disciplines of marketing or sales, but across the entire revenue performance spectrum. The concepts of Buyer Stages and Information Discovery were discussed at length in a previous chapter, but the remaining aspects of the framework deserve a closer look.

Known or Unknown Buyers

There are important differences between communicating with a prospective buyer whose name you have in a marketing database and an unknown prospect. While this observation seems trivial, in today's communications, there is a growing number of ways to identify prospective buyers. Likewise, each communication vehicle that requires a known buyer requires the buyer to be identified in a specific way.

Historically, the postal address was the relevant identifier. In recent years, the e-mail address became an equally, if not more, important identifier. Now, with an explosion of communication media, identifiers on Twitter, Facebook, LinkedIn, and other platforms are gaining in importance and may soon equal the importance of other identification methods.

It's important to examine whether each potential revenue investment relies on a known audience. If so, analyze the size and quality of that audience within the marketing database because it should drive any investment decision.

Paid *vs.* Earned Attention

To get the attention of prospects, marketers have traditionally invested in media purchases. Today, investments in attention are splitting into two basic groups:

- **Paid**
  In this model, the marketer invests cash directly in content and message distribution. A media buy is an initiative that involves mainly financial costs.

- **Earned**
  Prospects' attention is earned by creating relevant, interesting content. But it can also be *lost* through over-communication, poor targeting, or low-quality content. Content for a blog is an example of an earned media investment.

As markets and prospects increasingly gain control over the messages they receive and the content they pay attention to, the importance of earned media increases. Correspondingly, the impact of paid media decreases. Marketers must give careful consideration to how an audience's attention and permission to communicate are earned—and what actions can destroy that permission and trust.

No communication option is inherently more "right" or "wrong" than any other. Each option simply offers different economics and targets an audience in a slightly different manner. This must be considered when selecting communication options.

INVESTMENT OPTIONS

Every week, new investment options arise for generating revenue. At the same time, existing options evolve, and once-popular options sometimes fall out of favor, disappear, or change their entire approach. The following discussion, therefore, can be neither exhaustive nor definitive, as it is based on popular marketing options available as of this writing. Each may change or disappear, and new, more relevant options may appear. Likewise, there may be investment options for your business that do not appear here. This section also assumes a very basic familiarity with each platform, but does not assume a deep knowledge of each's intricacies.

Platts first sought to understand where their buyers were doing research and learning about the commodities industry. One of the first realizations they made was that a significant difference existed in the way that this discovery took place in different regions of the globe. In the emerging markets of India, China, and the Middle East, for example, where the culture is more oriented around face to face interactions, prospective buyers were more likely to attend conferences in order to learn about new approaches and techniques that would help them buy/sell/trade commodities in their job. In these markets, where buyers had typically bought and sold off of long term price contracts, the concepts Platts was introducing were relatively new, and education efforts focused on how to leverage new tools like using a publisher's spot pricing as a basis for negotiations.

In the more established market of North America, however, where spot trading was well established, Platts focused on guiding prospective buyers to investigate specific solutions that might be of interest to their business. If in a conversation with an existing account that worked with their oil products, a Platts representative detected a potential interest in gas products, the representative would add that buyer to a 6 month nurturing program to grow and explore this interest over time.

Case Example

When SolarWinds developed the first free tools that they offered to the network management community, they approached them with a marketing mindset. Rather than treat the free tools as second class citizens, they ensured that every tool was extremely high quality and solved a broadly relevant technical problem. This approach accomplished two things for SolarWinds. First, the ability to solve a broadly relevant technical problem meant that these tools drove broad adoption of the SolarWinds fee-based products once a user was introduced to the SolarWinds product family. Both directly via search, or through influencers in the industry, these tools were widely discussed, highly recommended, and became the standard among network engineers. Second, the investment in quality provided a strong validation of SolarWinds as a provider of quality network tools. When a buyer was considering one of the paid tools, their experience with the free tool quickly eliminated any of their questions around quality and performance.

Display Advertising

Display advertising is the quintessential broad communication tool. Whether in banner ads or billboards, it targets a demographic or firmographic segment with messaging that is most broadly applicable. Accordingly, display advertising shows a very low cost-per-"eyeball," but an equivalently low value, since very few of those who see the advertisement interact with it or act on it.

Viewers of display advertising are passive. They are not actively seeking the message they receive, and only interact if they discover that it is of interest. A key advantage is that there is no need to personally identify the recipient to have them view the ad. Also, there is a clear and proven financial model. Display advertising is most appropriate for the Awareness stage of the buying process.

Influencer-based Promotions

Services such as Klout are beginning to offer ways to identify and incent key influencers. By providing trials, briefings, and insider access to the individuals who influence a particular market area, marketers hope to provide an experience worth talking about. This area of marketing is undergoing rapid evolution as marketers, influencers, and technology platforms explore the careful balance between unbiased opinion and carefully structured incentives.

Done successfully, these incentives, often mainly financial in nature, can guide a set of key influencers to discuss, showcase, and potentially recommend your solution to their audience.

Social Question Sites

Social question-and-answer sites like Quora offer a way to engage not only with an audience that is actively seeking information by asking questions, but also an audience that is open to passively discovering information by noticing an interesting discussion thread.

Since these sites rely on active participation, the investment is generally one of time and effort to earn the attention of casual participants and directly engage with those asking questions.

Twitter and Facebook

Although Twitter and Facebook are very different platforms, and offer substantially different communication options, they fit a similar investment model for driving revenue. Both offer vehicles for sharing content that can be discovered by prospective buyers. This content can be valuable throughout the buying process, but is most often seen in the Awareness stage. As the marketers make connections with prospects, identities get established and captured. However, as a marketing initiative, neither Twitter nor Facebook require a database of names.

Unlike traditional media, however, the primary way to have your content shared broadly in either of these media is through third-party influencers. Although each platform is experimenting with paid advertising, the most effective way to leverage each platform remains the creation of great content, and developing strong relationships with influencers. Each of these efforts requires earning—rather than paying for—this attention. The relatively low investment/value of each interaction is appropriate for its typical use at the Awareness stage.

Direct Mail

In many ways, direct mail campaigns are similar to display advertising campaigns. The principal difference is that the targeted audience is based on a database of known names (that can be owned, purchased, or rented), rather than an online or offline traffic location. A direct mail campaign typically targets a definable demographic or firmographic segment with the type of broad messaging typical for engaging prospective buyers in the Awareness stage.

Since a direct-mail recipient is typically not actively seeking the message, the discovery of the information is passive and relies on the marketer to select and communicate a topic or a creative design that catches the recipient's attention at that moment. The investment in direct mail is almost purely financial, and typically has the low-cost, low-value profile of display advertising.

Tradeshow

A mainstay of business-to-business marketing, the tradeshow is a great environment for reaching buyers who are either unaware of your company and/or solution or who are looking for more information on what you can provide to companies like them. You do not need to know the attendees in advance, so it is an ideal opportunity to engage with a broader audience of interested potential buyers.

Tradeshows are attended by prospective buyers who actively seek information from vendors, so they represent a compelling investment option. The investment that is made is usually toward the middle of the spectrum of costs and value. The typical tradeshow is primarily a financial investment.

Webinars/Events

Another B2B marketing mainstay is the use of webinars or events to highlight specific topics, interesting use cases, case studies, or other topics that attract buying audiences in the Investigation stage. Since webinars and events are usually promoted directly to known audiences, they rely on the audience passively noticing something of interest in the topic being discussed. Many of these events are promoted to a "house list" as part of a nurture program, so the primary goal is earning the audience's attention and not losing it through over-communication.

Blogging

A business blog provides a forum to explore niche topics more deeply. Each post can explore a topic that provides details on how a particular client has used your solution, how a solution can be implemented in a specific vertical industry, or technical considerations for a particular use case. These niche topics are interesting to prospects in the Investigation phase of their buying process and who are exploring how the solution might be best applied.

The main investment in blogging is the time it takes to develop exceptional content and nurture the strong relationships that earn the attention of a loyal readers and influencers. This time investment can be significant, making blogging an investment that lies in the middle of the cost/value spectrum. The investment is crucial, however, because influencers can share your content, enabling your ultimate audience—which may not have been known to you in advance—to discover it.

Search Ads

Perhaps the most common way for marketers to identify and engage with buyers actively seeking information is through search. By aligning ads with the precise search terms prospective buyers use, you can find individuals who are actively seeking the information you provide. There is no need to know the individuals in advance, and the economics of search advertising can be reasonable in many cases. The investment is also purely a financial one.

The precise topics that prospective buyers are seeking information about align well with information that is relevant in the Investigation stage. Buyers want to understand more about the precise fit of a solution category within their business.

Nurture Campaigns

Lead-nurturing campaigns help you stay in contact with buyers who are a good fit but not currently showing interest. Careful topic selection keeps the audience engaged as they discover insights and new applications that are of interest to them and applicable to their business. As nurture campaigns communicate with previously

known individuals and usually use e-mail marketing as
the primary communication vehicle, they are an investment that requires audience permission, and hence are
very much an earned media investment.

Objection-Handling Tools

Objection-handling tools such as ROI calculators, objec-
tion-diffusing whitepapers, and customer testimonials
are often used near the close of the Investigation stage
and early in the Validation stage as prospects encounter
reasons for not moving forward. These content tools are
often presented directly to prospects who have shown
signs of an objection in the hope that they engage with
the information and resolve their objection.

Due to the limited audience scope, the cost-per-person
for tools is medium-high, but the value can be equally
significant as late-stage buying objections are resolved.
Although not truly a media type, these tools require
an investment of time to create sufficiently compelling
messaging that overcomes objections. As a result, they
function more like earned media than paid media.

Inbound Requests

To accommodate buyers actively seeking information,
most organizations create an inbound request process.
Typically, this function covers the "contact sales" form
on the website and the requester receives a follow-up
response via e-mail or phone. Since it is more labor-
intensive than presenting search ads, it is not only more
costly but also more valuable. Creating and optimizing a

good inbound request process usually requires a fair bit of time, and it serves the buyer who was not necessarily known previously. This buyer is usually in the latter stages of Investigation or early stages of Validation.

Free Trials

Like the inbound information request, a prospect requests a free trial of your company's solution. This is highly desirable because, for many organizations, the information that the prospect seeks is best provided by experiencing the solution itself. This allows those prospects, usually at the late stages of Investigation or early Validation stage, to try the solution in a time or functionally limited manner. The investment in this process is usually medium-high, but returns a high value because it earns the attention of well-qualified prospects.

Online Store

When buyers reach their own conclusions in the Validation stage, and require only the ability to execute a transaction, an online store is the right option. Online stores cater to those people—whether previously known or not—who are actively looking to finalize a transaction. It provides a medium-high level of value per person, for an equivalent level of investment. An online store relies on the prospect's earned attention, but is not a media type in itself.

Inside Sales

The complexities of most B2B sales cycles mean that most transactions can be completed only with the help of trained professionals who help the buyer navigate the challenging path to a completed transaction. This person-to-person interaction that guides each buyer through each challenge is at the highest end of the cost/value spectrum. Sales professionals provide this value by guiding motivations, sharing perspectives, orchestrating resources, and establishing evaluation frameworks.

It requires an investment in staffing to build an inside sales team that earns the right to continue the dialogue with the prospect by spending time to understand needs and communicate solutions. The inside sales model can, for certain products and sales cycles, provide a slight benefit over the field sales model. This is because most conversations take place over the phone and via Web conference, which is somewhat more efficient than face-to-face meetings.

Field Sales

This is similar to inside sales, but with the relationship-building advantage of spending time face-to-face with decision makers. Field sales professionals guide the enterprise buying process by developing personal relationships with key decision makers, detecting nuances of behavior that can only be seen face to face, and gaining critical insights through casual conversations with internal champions. As an investment, the field sales professional is both the most expensive, but also the most highly valued, on a per-person basis.

This chart shows a wide variety of options for investing in driving revenue. Each option may or may not be applicable for any given business, depending on where in the buying process the challenges are seen, what type of resources (cash or time) are available, and whether the right set of names exists to target people directly

Figure 4.2 – **Investments in Attention**

	Paid		Earned
Active	SEM		SEO
	Tradeshows		Quora participation
	Quora sponsorship		Twitter engagement
	iPhone app sponsorship		Support communities
			Inbound telesales
Passive	Advertising		Content marketing
	Tradeshows		LinkedIn Groups
	● Direct Mail		Viral videos
	Event sponsorship		● Email marketing
	Remarketing		Blogging
	● Appointment setting		● Sales calling campaigns
Influenced	Klout promotions		Word-of-Mouth marketing
	Foursquare promotions		Social Media relations
	Promoted tweets		Analyst relations
			● Reference program

Requires: ● Known Buyer

THE AGGREGATE EFFECT ON NATURAL SEARCH

Collectively, these investments let you share your content, ideas, and perspectives with a potential market. If the ideas are good, and your relationships are well-maintained, then the ideas will be shared with your influencers' audiences, and so on. However, this sharing leaves an important online footprint. Much, if not all, sharing of your information provides a digital audit trail. This record of content sharing is then tracked by the major search engines. This is not a book on search engine optimization, and the algorithms used by the search engines are not static, but the general dynamic is the important one. Search engines, as we've discussed previously, are inherently *social filters* of information. The more your content is shared, and the more it is shared by people who are deemed experts in your field, the higher it is ranked.

A high ranking in search engines is crucial to ensure that your message successfully reaches those who actively seek the information it provides.

A FRAMEWORK, NOT AN ANSWER

This view and analysis of revenue investments is only a framework that provides an understanding of existing options, and a way of thinking about future options. Each organization and, in fact, each product line has a unique market situation and requires you to choose investment alternatives with great care.

This framework is not a decision tree and does *not* attempt to make these decisions for you. Different investments achieve different goals within each unique business context. Apart from an investment in a corporate website, which makes sense for any business, each investment alternative may or may not make sense. However, in deconstructing your marketing goals, your buyer's propensity to actively seek or passively respond to messaging, and the available investment options, you are able to make informed decisions on which marketing and sales options make the most sense for you and your business.

> ### Case Example
>
> Search was a key component of how prospective buyers discovered what Platts could offer them, and the Platts team put an appropriate amount of effort into ensuring that they could be found. In providing a wealth of content that contributed to buyers awareness and investigation efforts, however, they noticed an interesting result. First, the context of how the information was discovered was important in analyzing conversion rates; while a buyer who navigated to a page on iron ore pricing from the main Platts web site would be able to understand it in context, a buyer who found that specific page via a search or a link from a partner site would not have the benefit of this context. The traffic to inquiry conversion rates reflected this lack of context. Therefore, Platts realized that they could not necessarily use the same page(s) for search landing pages which prompted them to create customized landing pages based on keywords and or banner ad locations.

FIVE

THE FOUNDATION OF THE REVENUE ENGINE

THE NEW DRIVE FOR HIGH QUALITY DATA

Building an effective, high-performance revenue engine requires the right frameworks, measurements, and efforts to engage with prospects and guide them through a buying process that they control. However, like any engine, it performs best when it's clean and well-tuned.

Figure 5.1

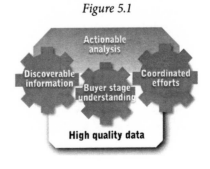

For a revenue engine, this means clean data, continual analysis and adjustment, and prompt response when the warning signs indicate that performance is beginning to suffer.

CLEAN DATA FOR GOOD PERFORMANCE

Perhaps the most important aspect of optimal revenue engine performance is the quality of your marketing database. Only with clean data can you effectively define and target segments of buyers. Only if the data is consistent can you easily build the rules you need for scoring and routing leads. Only if the data is standard and normalized can your marketing analytics give you the business insights you need to optimize your revenue engine.

The reason for the increased emphasis on data cleanliness is that all of the systems that enable us to understand our prospects, determine their location in the buying processes, and interact with them appropriately rely on automated systems driven by clean data. For these systems to perform optimally, data must conform to the 3 C's of data quality.

THE 3 C'S OF DATA QUALITY

The "3 C's" of data quality are the basic elements of clean data; consistency, completeness, and correctness. They help provide smooth performance in a revenue engine.

Consistency

Systems look at data in a very black and white manner. We can clearly see that "V.P. Marketing," "VP Marketing," "Vice Pres Mktg," and "Vice President of Marketing" are all the same title and department. But to an automated system, they are distinct and different. To use this data within a rules-based system, such as scoring, personalization, or analysis, either each rule must take into account all possible permutations of the data, or the data must be made consistent prior to use.

Similarly, if the data on an individual, his interests, or the company he works for is not in one place and consistently managed, it becomes difficult for systems or analytics to understand what is taking place. If there are, for example, duplicate or triplicate records for one individual, each of which contains missing or inconsistent data, it will be difficult—if not impossible—to personalize messages to that individual based on his interests or buying role.

Complete

If the data on a company's industry or size, or an individual's role, geography, or title is missing, it prevents us from correctly understanding who the buyer is and where he or she is in the buying process. Granted, a complete profile can be difficult and/or prohibitively expensive to gather from a prospective buyer at first meeting. However, it can be assembled and aggregated over time using a variety of sources and techniques to generate a very accurate picture.

Correct

Incorrect data is equally detrimental to the effectiveness of a revenue engine. People change jobs, addresses, contact information, and roles. Organizations expand and may change industries, grow revenues, or move into new markets and territories. Maintaining correct data, through both selective sourcing from accurate data providers, and direct engagement with website visitors to correct or confirm their data, is a key to smooth performance of the revenue engine.

These 3 C's form the foundation that drives all aspects of marketing and selling in a more effective and efficient manner. With normalized data, the ease and accuracy of building precise market segments increases dramatically, often resulting in 10 to 20 times the number of contacts in a segment compared to poorly normalized data. With consistent data, you can personalize content by industry, which is a powerful and effective marketing technique. With correct data, you know that a single, accurate, up-to-date record exists for each company and contact in your database, so you can analyze performance without errors. With complete data, the insights into each person's role, stage, and interest in the buying process become evident, and allow accurate assessment of when sales is best to engage with the prospect.

While sales teams in many organizations wrestle with the challenges of data quality, this focus has generally not moved as far up the revenue funnel as it must. Maintaining a high level of data quality requires more diligence than many marketing organizations are used to. This is because of the nature of the data sources that today's marketers work with.

MANAGING DATA SOURCES

Understanding where the data comes from, and in what form, provides insights into the challenges of improving its quality. Marketing data typically comes from many different sources, each of which has unique challenges:

- **Remote Systems**
  Marketing often obtains data from CRM systems, data warehouses, or customer data masters. This data is often imported and loaded into a marketing database on a nightly (or more frequent) basis, and integrated into existing marketing data. In many cases, there is only a limited opportunity to change the format or quality of the original data, and it must be dealt with automatically each time it is imported. While the data in remote systems may be cleansed, it may not conform to the standards in your marketing database.

- **Continual Sources**
  Some sources of data—such as Web forms, trade-show leads, webinar registrants, and trial down-loaders—contribute a steady flow of data to the marketing database. The continual nature of these sources means any data cleansing must be done continually, and thus automatically, to avoid

allowing this steady flow of data to begin dirtying
the overall database.

- **Controlled** *vs.* **Non-Controlled**
  Many of the sources you deal with are not within
  your control, such as lists from tradeshows, business
  cards, and many Web forms. The data from them is
  of varying quality and formats.

Since there are a variety of data sources that interact
with your revenue engine, a single attempt to control
them all is futile. Many sources add data that, un-
cleansed, would quickly erode the quality, reliability, and
performance of the entire database. The foundation of
revenue performance would suffer greatly. The real-time
nature of many of these sources of data, however, means
they must be cleansed "inline." The batch-based, offline,
bulk processes for cleaning data no longer work in today's marketing environment.

THE CONTACT WASHING MACHINE

The most common method for cleansing data today is
manual, one-time processes, where a marketing database is processed, either by a specialized agency or a
dedicated software application. During this process, the
full data set is processed, cleansed, de-duplicated, and
returned to the marketing database in pristine form.
The challenge with this approach is that the data sources
we are dealing with are operating continually. Every

Web form, upload, registration, data pull from CRM, or manual edit changes and "contaminates" your marketing data.

Yes, you may be able to control some data sources, but many you cannot. If a data source contributes dirty data, your marketing database will soon have a significant percentage of data that cannot be relied upon. The only viable solution is to automate the data cleansing at every touch point using what can be described as a "contact washing machine." Each time that data is sourced or changed, via Web forms, uploads, or edits, it must undergo the cleansing process of the contact washing machine to remain clean and standardized.

The contact washing machine process runs automatically, with no human involvement, to manage and maintain the quality of data in your marketing database. The exact configuration of the contact washing machine will vary from business to business, but, in general, will do the following:

- Normalize titles, roles, industries, countries, and other data requiring consistency against a common reference set.

- Standardize data such as revenue ranges and employee sizes so it is appropriately set up for segmentation and analytics.

- Identify and manage duplicates so that each person and company is only represented once.

- Correct any data based on internal or external sources.

- Remove any data that appears to be deliberately invalid, such as "aaaa," "555-1212," or "test@test.com."

- Append any data, such as company information, that can be discovered from external sources.

In addition, of course, a contact washing machine can perform any industry- or business-specific data management tasks necessary to cleanse and manage the data.

Bulk data cleansing, while unable to meet the real-time needs of today's marketers, does offer additional advanced cleansing capabilities. If you think of clean data as the oil that keeps your revenue engine running smoothly, think of bulk data cleansing as an oil change, and the contact washing machine is the oil filter within the engine. A periodic oil change may do more to clean the oil, but you won't get far from the mechanic's garage if your engine does not have an oil filter to keep things continually cleansed.

Data and the User Experience

With data sources that are both user-facing, and within your control, such as Web forms and event registrations, you need a careful balance between data quality and the user experience. This is particularly true when it comes to semi-standard data such as title or industry. On one side of the spectrum, the best experience for the user is often free-form text. Forcing a user to select from a defined set of choices often leads to a frustrating experi-ence. A short list of titles, for example, will often lack a good match for the person's title. However, a longer list forces the visitor to select from too many options, and impacts his ability to quickly use the form.

On the opposite side of the spectrum, a high-perfor-mance revenue engine relies on standard, formatted, structured data that is best sourced from a standardized list of values in a pick-list. So, how do you balance the requirement for the best possible visitor experience with the need for cleansed, structured data that works best within your marketing database? The answer is through using a secondary process to parse the user's input into secondary data fields for normalized data.

With this technique, the site visitor enters free-form data into the Web form, which provides an optimal user experience. As the free-text form is submitted, the contact washing machine scrubs the data. The free-form text is compared to a standard list of titles to determine the best possible match. Since this step is automated, and not part of the user experience, the size of the list of titles does not matter and accuracy does not have to be sacrificed.

After a match is made, the resulting data can be fed into one or more secondary fields, rather than back into the original field, leaving the user's free-form data intact. In many cases, it may be useful to feed the data into more than one field. For example, when parsing a title, it may be useful to split it into a "level" component (Vice President, C-level, Manager, Director), and a "department" component (sales, marketing, finance, human resources). For instance:

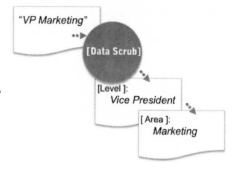

Figure 5.2 – **The Contact Washing Machine**

- User input: "V.P. Marketing"

- Raw title is maintained as "V.P. Marketing"

- Level is standardized as "Vice President"

- Role is standardized as "Marketing"

With a structured title and normalized data, we can confidently and accurately apply our rules for managing, communicating with, and nurturing the user.

ASKING FOR DATA—PROGRESSIVE PROFILING

The final aspect of ensuring your revenue engine uses the best possible data is to ensure that you optimize each buyer interaction and request for data. Many studies show, and intuition confirms, that large registration forms discourage prospective buyers, especially in the early stages of the buying process. However, the more we seek to understand the role, motivations, and interests of each buyer, the more information we need. While much of this information can be captured or deduced based on their digital body language, the explicit information captured in Web forms is also extremely valuable.

To derive maximum value from each Web form interaction, we must balance three variables to optimize the user's experience against our need for information:

- **Value of the Asset**
  Before a prospective buyer submits information, he must perceive that he will receive something of value in return. Unfortunately, as information becomes progressively more freely available, this perceived value continues to decrease. Marketers must continually fine-tune the amount and quality of information, if any, they ask for based on the assets they provide in exchange. "Landing page to asset conversion" rates are a good indicator. If the conversion rate is too low, the amount of information being requested may be too high. Typically, product data sheets, marketing promotions, and company information are not perceived as valuable enough by the prospect to merit his submitting information. However, research reports, webinars with industry luminaries, and face-to-face events often are worth the time for the prospect. Each marketing asset requires a value assessment to see how much visitor information can be obtained.

- **Currently Known Information**
  Each question decreases response rates, so repeating the same question when subsequent assets are requested is a recipe for failure. It is critical to understand who each visitor is and what you already know about him. This lets you optimize his access to your information without unnecessary barriers.

- **Required Information**
  In parallel, understanding and carefully restricting what information you require lets you minimize the visitor's burden. For example, do you really need a fax number? Even if it's an optional field, it makes the Web form longer and less appealing. Similarly, consider skipping company information such as industry, revenue, or size. You might be able to source that information elsewhere.

After assessing these criteria, you can streamline each Web form to minimize your information request. With each interaction, only request new, incremental information not currently known, and gradually move toward a complete and carefully chosen profile.

6

SIX

THE COURAGE TO MAKE HARD DECISIONS

A FRAMEWORK FOR ANALYZING REVENUE

With the foundations of revenue performance management in place, let's begin to build a comprehensive analysis framework around the revenue engine. This framework shows us where investments are having an effect and where new ones are needed. It does so in a way that shows us why buyers are buying, how many

can be expected to buy in the current quarter as well as future quarters, and what investments would change these patterns. This framework gives us the courage to make the hard decisions regarding where to invest in our revenue engines.

THE FRAMEWORK OF THE BUYING PROCESS

The first step is to build a single version of the truth for our internal understanding of where a prospect is in the buying process. At the highest level, as we've seen, our view of the buyer shows some distinct transitions:

- **Unknown to Known**
  As buyers move from the early stages of Awareness and Education into either deeper Education or early stage Investigation, they often become known to us.

- **Known to Qualified**
  As buyers engage with marketing, their behavior may show that they have become sufficiently interested. They are qualified as leads and passed to the sales team.

- **Qualified to Closed**
  The sales team follows a process to ensure that the opportunity moves effectively toward a close.

However, within each of these sections, a secondary level of understanding is applied.

Understanding the Unknown

Understanding Awareness

One of the most difficult tasks for marketers is understanding the somewhat intangible effects of awareness and education efforts. Efforts to "build buzz," "generate interest," or "get the word out" can be frustratingly difficult to measure. Nonetheless, there is a strong consensus that these efforts are essential to downstream successes. To establish a measurement framework, we must first evaluate some of the tools we explored earlier that address unknown prospects (who are usually at the Awareness or early Investigation stages of their buying processes). Looking at the set of available investment options for building awareness in the unknown end of the buyer spectrum, the investment framework can be simplified to the following:

Figure 6.2 – **Investment Options**

Investments	Paid	Earned
Active	**SEM:** ad budget **Tradeshow:** Sponsorship budget **iPhone:** App development	**SEO:** Content creation/optimization **Tradeshow:** Team time/effort **Twitter:** Interaction time/effort **Support:** Team time
Passive	**Advertising:** Ad budget **Tradeshow:** Sponsorship budget **Direct Mail:** Print, mail, and list costs **Events:** Sponsorship budget **Remarketing:** Ad budget **Appointment Setting:** Pay per appt.	**Content:** Creation/promotion **LinkedIn:** Question answering **Viral Video:** Video creation **Email Marketing:** Content/offer creation **Blogging:** Content creation **Sales:** Calling Campaign time
Influenced	**Klout promotions:** Giveaways **Foursquare promotions:** Giveaways **Promoted Tweet:** Ad budget	**Word-of-Mouth:** Relationship effort **Social Media:** Influencer relationship effort **Analyst relations:** Analyst time **Reference Program:** Client relationships

When driving Awareness and early-stage Investigation within this group, the first angle to analyze is the natural potential for generating awareness in each category. If, for example, only 1,000 people per month actively search for a particular term, that becomes the maximum potential of your efforts to optimize against that search term.

When investing in these categories, success comes down to either traffic that was driven to take action because they find the content interesting, or the community that is now being influenced in the direction of your message.

Figure 6.3 – **Audience Measures**

Audience	Paid	Earned
Active	**Search**: On-topic Searches **Tradeshow**: Attendance **iPhone**: App downloads	Search: On-topic Searches Tradeshow: Attendance Twitter: Followers Support: Community size
Passive	**Advertising**: Available inventory **Tradeshow**: Attendees **Direct Mail**: List size **Event**: Potential attendees **Remarketing**: Target group size **Appointments**: List size	**Content Marketing:** Long-tail searches **LinkedIn**: Group sizes **Viral Videos**: unclear **Email Marketing**: List size **Blogging**: Long-tail searches **Sales Calling Campaigns**
Influenced	**Klout**: Influential personalities **Foursquare**: Geolocal traffic **Promoted Tweets:** Influencer Follower counts	**Word-of-Mouth:** Interested Community size **Social Media:** Interested community size **Analyst relations:** Analyst audience **Reference program:** Active sales opportunities

Figure 6.4 – **Result Metrics**

Results	Paid		Earned	
Active	**Search:** Referred traffic **Tradeshow:** Booth traffic **iPhone:** App users		**Search:** Referred traffic **Tradeshow:** Booth traffic **Twitter:** Referred traffic **Support Community:** Community traffic	
Passive	**Ads:** Referred traffic **Tradeshow:** booth traffic **Direct Mail:** call-to-action traffic **Events:** attendance **Remarketing:** Referred traffic **Appt Setting:** Appointments		**Natural search traffic** to long-tail content **LinkedIn:** Referred traffic **Video:** Video views **Email:** Views and traffic **Blog:** Natural search traffic to blog content **Sales Calling:** Conversations	
Influenced	**Klout:** Web traffic driven by influencers **Foursquare:** Check-ins **Promoted Tweets:** Referred traffic		**Word-of-Mouth:** Non-referred traffic **Social Media:** Traffic referred by influencers **Analyst relations:** Referred traffic, rankings **Reference program:** Reference count	

Although it is an inexact science, measuring your revenue team's performance against their goals of generating awareness and influence in the market is the only way to ensure that your revenue funnel does not go dry.

Re-engaging Inactive Buyers

An optimized revenue engine often shows an interesting set of buyer dynamics at the top of the funnel. For instance, just having a contact's name in your marketing database does not in any way imply interest. That name might be someone from several years ago who has not shown interest in recent years. There may be names that were entered from a list purchase who have never shown interest. Although these are "known" prospects, they lack any signs of interest and we must engage with them

Figure 6.5 – Re-engaging Inactive Buyers

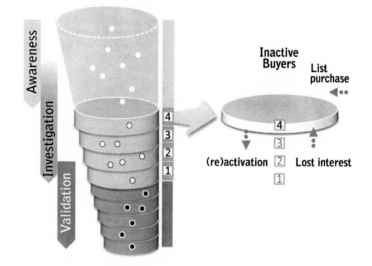

as we would unknown prospects who have never shown any interest.

It is critical to carve out these "inactive names" from the top of the funnel when looking at analytics. Otherwise, our measurements and assessments of campaigns targeting the top of the funnel (and also the overall funnel conversion metrics) become improperly skewed.

The best way to account for this is to rigorously eliminate inactive names from the "aware," "interested," or "engaged" stages at the top of the funnel. If a lead, even one who was once interested, has made no inquiries and taken no actions in a period of time (depending on your sales model, it might be three months), you should return that lead to the inactive lead pool. What's more, by defining an "inactive" group at the top of your marketing funnel, you can better understand the effects of awareness and nurturing campaigns in new ways.

Figure 6.6 – **Qualifying the Known**

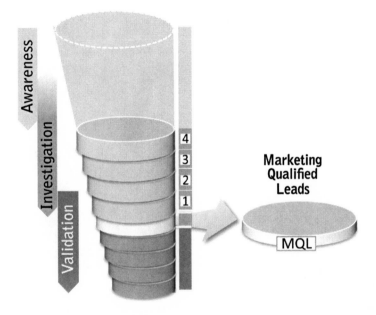

Qualifying the Known

Once a prospect is known, when does it make sense to pass that lead over to sales? What is the process for having sales take a qualified lead and engage in a sales conversation? This hand-off process is one of the most critical in the entire revenue engine and warrants a deeper investigation.

Figure 6.7 – Fit, Engagement, and Lead Qualification

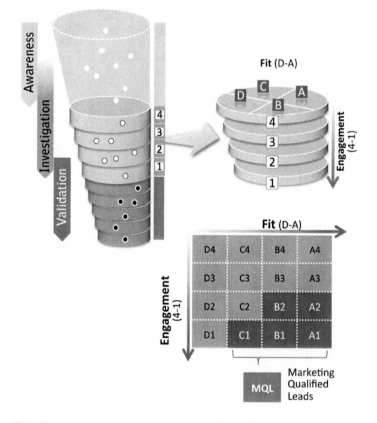

Fit, Engagement, and Lead Qualification

Savvy sales executives recognize that all of the interest in
the world is meaningless if that prospect lacks the ability
to finalize a purchase transaction for his organization.
Qualification of "fit"—confirming the individual is the
right person, with sufficient seniority, in an organization
of sufficient size in the right industry—is equally critical
to engagement.

However, although both of these dimensions—"fit" and "engagement"—are equally important, they are two entirely distinct aspects of lead qualification that must be considered separately in assessing whether sales involvement is warranted. Fit, as a dimension, is something that can mainly be assessed based on explicit criteria that does not change significantly over time. The data on role, title, company size, geography, and industry can usually be gathered through Web forms and standard

Case Example

With buyers being nurtured to grow their interest in Platts solutions, the team focused on detecting the signals that indicated a likely buyer. Existing customers were analyzed utilizing a lead scoring process to look for patterns in industry, role, and organization size was analyzed to understand what most correlated with a viable opportunity being created. Surprisingly to the team, engagement was a much stronger predictor of purchase than fit indicators such as industry and title. At the same time, the Platts team noticed that specific pieces of content could give clear indications of buying process stage. For example, a person viewing a whitepaper on "Criteria for evaluating an Iron Ore provider" was likely to be at the "Evaluating options" stage of their buying process. Engagement indicators that took effort on the part of the prospect, such as filling out a lengthy web form, also showed a strong propensity to indicate purchase intent. Platts utilized this data to form their lead scoring program. They first ran it only in Eloqua where only the marketers could view the results allowing them to tweak the scoring program before introducing to sales.

data sources, and can be expected to remain static over a few quarters or a year.

With a lead score applied to each dimension, we can build a fit/engagement matrix. The value of the lead's fit can be mapped to a standard definition of A, B, C, or D, where A is a high fit, and D is a low fit. Similarly for a lead's engagement, we apply the standard definition of 1, 2, 3, or 4 that we discussed earlier.

The sales team can then understand leads as A1s, C3s, or B4s, etc. The underlying scoring definition of what earns a lead points, how those points are adjusted over time, and which range of points maps to each rank, need not be visible to the sales team at large. A core group of key individuals within sales and marketing can debate the definitions and make necessary adjustments each quarter.

Now, with a clear definition of each lead and its location in the qualification matrix, we can structure a new relationship between marketing and sales. The discussion can turn to which leads should move from marketing to sales, and to which sales team if there are multiple teams. In other words—we are defining an MQL. A1 leads are obviously passed directly to sales—likely to a field sales force. But we need a mapping for where other leads go. Some should be passed to an inside sales team, some might go to a partner channel, and some may be retained for further nurturing.

This split between the underlying details of lead qualification, and the high-level funnel metric of MQLs allows you to account for the reality that not all interested buyers will truly be able to purchase, and not all ideal prospects are interested.

Making the Transition

When, after careful analysis of both fit and engagement, a MQL is identified, significant work still remains to close a deal. The business pain must be fleshed out in more detail, internal stakeholders must reach consensus that your solution is the correct one, and terms and conditions must be agreed to. While marketing can do a lot to nurture and build interest, any potential sale of significant size requires a skilled sales professional to manage the people and politics that are involved in guiding a prospect to close.

Before the MQL enters the sales process, it must first make the transition to sales qualified opportunity (SQO). This interesting transition involves the lead moving from the generalized qualification criteria that sales and marketing have previously defined to the identification of a specific sales opportunity worth pursuing. This is best approached in two steps: First the MQL must be accepted by sales as a Sales Accepted Lead (SAL), and then that SAL must be confirmed as a Sales Qualified Opportunity (SQO).

The transition to an SAL requires sales to take a deeper look at the demographics, firmographics, and digital body language of the lead to determine if the automated rules for identifying an MQL have identified a truly worthwhile lead. Repeated challenges or objections from the sales team in this transition to an SAL may indicate that the definition of an MQL is not accounting for a certain pattern of interest. (For example, job seekers may show extensive Web activity, but are not truly qualified leads, and should be excluded).

Once we have an SAL, an initial conversation is needed to confirm that a buying opportunity exists. Historically, this first conversation may have been the first true significant exchange of information. Today, educated buyers are generally much more sophisticated regarding what they are looking for. What used to be called a "discovery" call, is different today. Savvy sales pros realize the education process has already progressed much further. In this initial conversation, the sales professional wants to determine whether a viable buying opportunity exists to commit sales resources. If so, the buying opportunity moves into the sales process as a Sales Qualified Opportunity (SQO).

Closing Deals

A sales process is merely the collection of activities that most reliably contribute to a successful sale. These activities focus on converting an SQO into a signed commercial agreement. We call these activities a process because they occur in an expected order that varies based on the sales strategy that works best for each company. From an evangelical sales strategy to product, solution, and provocation, each sales strategy dictates the order of activities. For example, in a product sales strategy, the demonstration occurs much earlier than in a solution sales strategy. In a provocation-based sales strategy, you might never demonstrate your product.

Activities executed in a defined sequence are the essence of a sales process. There are three important aspects. First, the sales team defines the activities that it executes to ensure the right conversations are happening. Second, we must define the activities we expect the client to perform to ensure that the buyer's interest is progressing in the right direction. Third, we must define the specific, verifiable, customer-focused outcomes that are the basis for moving from one phase of the sales process to another. Without defined prospect activities and verifiable outcomes, we can only measure our own effort, but not results.

At each stage, we must also carefully observe the buyer's online behavior to identify signs that indicate he is, indeed, in that stage. This behavior differs from solution to solution, but it forms a powerful point of cross reference to validate assumptions. These observations of digital body language validate or challenge the assertions that we have made about the prospect activities and verifiable outcomes.

Although companies have varying numbers of stages in their sales processes, generally there are three major phases: assessing the fit, developing an answer, and completing a commercial agreement.

A generic sales process may look like the following:

E—Needs Analysis

(Will the solution make a difference for this customer?)

Sales Activities

- Identify decision-maker and/or internal champion
- Conduct initial discovery call
- Identify potential competition
- Confirm availability of budget
- Confirm ultimate decision-maker or contract signer
- Identify unique capability needed by the client

Prospect's Activities

- Identify and agree to access to decision-maker
- Participate in a discovery call
- Communicate an evaluation plan/process
- Confirm that project is budgeted or that budget approval is part of process
- Agree to a joint opportunity development process

Verifiable Outcomes

- "We have a problem that I think you can help us solve."

Observable Digital Body Language

- A shift from viewing thought-leadership and high-level content to more tactical content

- Search for lists of solutions or comparison guides

- Social media interaction, looking for peer recommendations

D—Solution Presentation

(Establish the value that the prospect will defend.)

Sales Activities

- Identify compelling event

- Map and identify business challenges and goals

- Map and communicate success criteria or proof points

- Identify internal champion

- Confirm executive sponsor

- Confirm the business or economic value or our unique capability

Prospect Activities

- Communicate business challenges and goals including functional requirements

- Agree to success criteria or proof points

- Identify executive sponsor and agree to provide access to executive sponsor

- Ensure that sponsor/decision-maker has confirmed that key business drivers and value have been addressed

Verifiable Outcomes

- "We agree on the business challenges, goals, and success criteria or proof points."
- "I will defend this decision because I agree with the economic or business value of your differentiation."
- "If you demonstrate those, we will move forward."

Observable Digital Body Language

- Internal champion forwards information to other team members
- Viewing of content that explains concepts to other stakeholders
- Activity and engagement seen from decision maker

C—Solution Proposal

(Confirm solution and articulate value in proposal.)

Sales Activities

- Present final solution scenario to evaluation team
- Submit formal written proposal
- Submit implementation plan

- Review and confirm business case/ROI with prospect
- Gain agreement on all steps in buying process by mapping out a mutually agreeable closing plan

Prospect Activities

- Agree to present business/economic value to the economic buyer
- Confirm as a "short list" vendor
- Participate in scoping exercise to help create implementation plan
- Identify all steps in buying process and agree to closing plan
- Initiate/finalize approval process

Verifiable Outcomes

- "We agree on the differentiation and value your solution brings."
- "You have successfully shown us you can deliver against the previously identified business/economic value."

Observable Digital Body Language

- ROI studies and calculators viewed
- Activity from a broader team as more people join the consensus

- Searches and social media activity seeks to find cost comparisons

B—Commitment and Negotiation

(Agreement to move forward as selected vendor)

Sales Activities

- Submit contractual terms
- Engage legal team for contract negotiations
- Negotiate price and terms

Prospect Activities

- Confirm selection as vendor either orally or in writing
- Initiate legal and/or procurement process
- Re-conform contract signer

Verifiable Outcomes

- "We have selected you as our vendor and we will sign agreements."

Observable Digital Body Language

- Teams involved in selecting, implementing, or using are looking at implementation and user information
- Legal and procurement teams may show some online activity

A—Closed/Won

- Contracts signed and delivered

Collectively, this objectively defined process for finalizing a sales transaction allows us to understand not just how buyers move through these stages, but, more importantly, what messages we must deliver to ensure that buyers are optimally prepared to engage with the sales team at each step.

TRUE VALUE AND TRUE COSTS

Every effective marketing or sales investment helps buyers navigate a buying process that moves them from the earliest stages of awareness to the final closing. To compare these investments, and make difficult decisions on where to invest in further and where to pull back, we need a framework for assessing the true value of buyers at each stage and the true cost of each investment.

Many digital initiatives have costs that are less clear than their television, print, or radio predecessors. What's more, the illusion of free can obscure very real costs. Likewise, the value created by each marketing initiative can be difficult to quantify—especially those not targeted at directly triggering a purchase event or qualifying a lead. By understanding these true costs and true value, we can better assess our marketing performance.

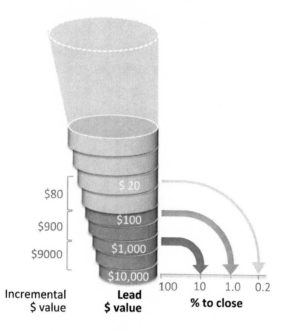

Figure 6.8 – The Value of a Lead

The Value of a Lead

In short buying cycles, where the transaction is quick and simple, the value of a marketing campaign can be measured directly. For example, a marketing campaign leads to a website visit. A product is added to the visitor's shopping cart, and the transaction is completed. Tying the buying event to that marketing campaign is both easy and sensible. Various marketing campaigns can be analyzed to see which offer and which creative execution drive more revenue.

However, with longer B2B buying cycles, this analysis is not as simple. Prospects move through the buying process at their own pace, facilitated by marketing messages and campaigns, but not explicitly driven by them. Some campaigns may generate broad awareness, some might educate on criteria to consider, and some might trigger buying actions directly. All are valuable, but measuring their value requires a different approach than we would use for simple sales cycles. We must associate a value with leads at each stage in the buying process and then analyze how successful we are at moving the leads to the next step of the process.

Using the framework we have created, with defined buying stages and objectively scored assessments of when buyers are at which stages, we can begin to assess value. With the buying stages defined, it's now possible to look at historical conversion rates to understand the implied value of a lead at each stage.

For example, if a deal is worth $10,000, and an MQL has a 10 percent conversion-to-close rate, it is worth (has an implied value of) $1,000. Similarly, if a lead at the "aware" stage has a 1 percent chance of converting, it is worth $100, and if an "inactive" name that has not yet shown any interest has a 0.2 percent chance of turning into revenue, it is worth $20 per name.

Note that these values are based on the conversion rate of the stage *through to close,* rather than conversion to the next stage.

Campaigns, Transitions, and Value

With value-per-stage established, we can finally see the value of a buyer's movement through the funnel—even if it does not directly translate to closed business or qualified leads being passed to sales. For example, if a buyer moves from "aware" ($100/lead) to "marketing qualified lead" ($1,000/lead), their value has increased by $900. Similarly, if a buyer moves from "inactive" ($20/lead) to "aware" ($100/lead), their value has increased by $80. If net new leads enter the funnel, and are deemed to be "aware," they are immediately worth $100.

Many campaigns target top-of-funnel or mid-funnel outcomes. Generating new names, educating buyers, establishing evaluation criteria, and nurturing buyers are all very valuable activities. However, they can be extremely difficult to measure unless there is a framework to assign value to each of the early stages.

What Causes What?

When measuring the effect of a marketing effort on buyer behavior, the first challenge is to determine the cause. Our understanding of where the prospect is in her buying process is derived from an overall understanding of her online behavior, interactions, and role within the organization. This is an aggregate measurement that combines a variety of influences and actions. A well-timed, compelling, and highly relevant marketing touch point may facilitate her moving to the next stage of her buying process. But our determination of that transition is based on looking at her overall behavior, rather than the one specific touch-point.

Put more simply, seeing a prospect click on a whitepaper can mean many things, depending on what we observe next. If the prospect was already known to be at the "aware" stage and the click on the whitepaper was not followed by any further activity, the click on the white-paper did not change this determination and did not cause forward motion in the buying process.

However, if she was originally inactive, and shortly after downloading the whitepaper, she performed actions and research that indicate she was found to be highly "in-terested", we can conclude that the whitepaper "caused" that transition.

To confirm this causality, we must look at two things: which marketing actions influenced a prospect, and how can those influences be linked to changes in the buyer's stage of the buying process?

Influence Threshold

In general, each marketing media type has its own threshold that allows us to conclude that the marketing action truly influenced its recipient. For e-mail market-ing, it may be a clickthrough on an e-mail. For direct mail, typing in a personalized URL (PURL) to visit a customized website is a sufficient threshold to define influence. For Twitter or Facebook, it is the clicking of a link.

Causality Measurement

With these influence thresholds defined, we can look at any transitions that a buyer made in her buying process and determine whether any of those marketing influences "caused" that transition. If the most recent influence occurs within a defined period of time, usually a week, prior to the stage transition, it can be deemed to have caused the transition.

The Cost of Earning Attention

In Chapter 4, we discussed the spectrum of potential revenue investments available. Some were investments of cash for paid media, while others were investments of time and effort for earned media. Quantifying the cost of financial investments is relatively straightforward, but quantifying the cost of earning attention is significantly more complicated.

Earned attention has two main cost components: getting attention, and keeping it. Both of these cost components can be significant, and easily on par with your expenditures for paid media. However, when only financial metrics are considered, many media types, especially digital ones, can appear to be almost "free."

This mindset—that a "free" communication vehicle such as e-mail can be used without cost—is a dangerous misconception. Even marketers who are sensitive to e-mail recklessness sometimes face internal pressure, such as an end-of-year revenue push, to send "one last blast to the entire database" with the justification that "it doesn't

cost us anything." This false impression often leads to
over-communication that, in turn, triggers diminished
response rates, spam complaints, and unsubscribes—all
signs that the audience's attention has begun to wane.

Figure 6.9 – **True Cost of an Email Campaign**

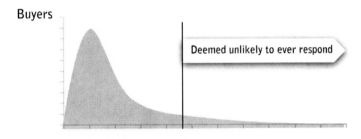

# of communication attempts

The True Cost of an E-Mail Campaign

To calculate the true cost of audience permission, we
need a frameworks that accounts for both getting and
losing the attention of those in the audience.

Getting Attention

At one end of the spectrum are the net new names entering your database, or inactive names being reactivated.
As a marketing team, you work hard to populate your
database—attending shows and events, putting on
webinars, publishing research, and investing in paid
and natural search. Each of these efforts, with varying
degrees of success, brings new names to your marketing
database. Let's look at the investment it takes to create
these marketing programs, and then divide that cost by
the number of net new names in your database, giving

Figure 6.10 – Calculating the True Cost of a Campaign

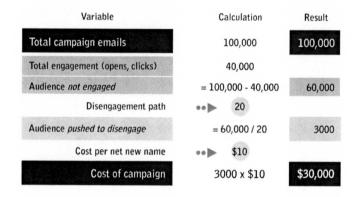

Variable	Calculation	Result
Total campaign emails	100,000	100,000
Total engagement (opens, clicks)	40,000	
Audience *not engaged*	= 100,000 - 40,000	60,000
Disengagement path	20	
Audience *pushed to disengage*	= 60,000 / 20	3000
Cost per net new name	$10	
Cost of campaign	3000 x $10	$30,000

us a Cost per Net New Name—the cost to get attention. For the sake of this calculation, let's assume that cost is $10.

Losing Attention

At the other end of the spectrum are the people who are disengaging from your messaging. This "emotional unsubscribe"—the reflexive ignoring or deleting of your messages—can be measured by looking at whether the recipient has become inactive. Measure whether the recipient has given your message any attention at all—e-mail opens, clicks, or website visits—in the past three or four months. If not, they have likely disconnected from your communications.

The Path to Disengagement

Between these two ends of the spectrum is what marketers control. Irrelevant messaging, poorly targeted content, and thinly disguised sales pitches quickly drive your audience away. To understand how long it takes for prospects to disengage, analyze your e-mail marketing history. Look at the number of "ignored" e-mails between any two "non-ignored" e-mails. If you look at a "reasonable maximum" for this number—say the 80th percentile—you can see how long it takes a person to disengage. For example, if only 20 percent of your audience ever re-engages after they have ignored 20 e-mails in a row, your Disengagement Path is 20 e-mails. Let's use this figure for our example.

Calculating a Real Cost of Earned Attention

With these two values, you can calculate the true cost of an e-mail campaign based on the value of earned attention. People who disengage must be replaced with net new names, or your overall effective marketing database shrinks. So, for an e-mail campaign sent to 100,000 people, of whom 40,000 open it, we have 60,000 who did not engage in any way.

To understand how many people this campaign likely caused to disengage, divide the total, 60,000, by the Disengagement Path of 20. If it takes 20 poorly targeted e-mails to cause one person to disengage, then each campaign causes 1/20 of its audience to disengage. By this calculation, this e-mail campaign disengaged 3,000 people. At a cost per net new name of $10, the cost to replace those pushed to disengage is $30,000—the hidden cost of this campaign.

This example looks at earned attention within a marketing database that nurtures prospective buyers via e-mail. However, calculating the cost of earning, and most importantly keeping, the attention of an audience is a common one across all media types.

The Cost of Being Engaged

Another cost of today's marketing efforts that is often disguised is the time it takes to remain engaged, via social media, with a market audience. While the hard costs are often very low, the time and energy investment is significant. Historically, marketing budgets have been evaluated and analyzed in terms of the external spend on media buys, creative, and events. This framework is no longer valid because engaging with influencers and prospective buyers takes significant amounts of direct time and effort from internal staff.

For a marketing organization focused on engaging buyers, we must begin to track the time spent as a relevant cost because this crucial marketing effort does not follow the traditional model of external spending that other marketing initiatives tend to follow.

Content Creation

Similarly, to engage buyers and influencers and ensure we are as "discoverable" as possible, we must devote significant time and energy to the creation of insightful, shareable content. Even though these are often internally generated materials, these content-creation costs can, and should, be measured specifically as a line item.

Figure 6.11 – The Content Gap

The Content Gap

In measuring these expenditures, however, we often uncover a content gap. Marketing is generally comfortable
producing content that focuses on awareness, education,
and brand preference. Also, in a sales support capacity,
marketing typically creates sales content, much of which
is used later in the buying process and is not necessarily
widely shared due to its direct selling nature.

It's that middle stage, however, where an interesting content creation (and cost measurement) challenge arises.
In the Investigation stage, buyers seek to understand
which solutions best match their business challenges.

Prospective buyers become aware of the solution category and the problems that it solves, and begin to understand that your organization may have a solution. At this phase, they are formulating plans for solving the business pain that you solve, discovering vendors to investigate further, and scoping the breadth and depth of the initiative in question. In this stage, deeper and more specific "best practice" content is often most useful.

The content that best meets the needs of this audience comes from your services team, subject matter experts, product consultants, designers, specialists, or engineers. These are the people with the knowledge, expertise, and passion to write about your solutions and what they can accomplish, the challenges and considerations, and what others in the industry are doing. This is non-salesy, informative content, but it is more detailed than the high-level thought leadership material that is appropriate at the Awareness stage.

Assistance from Subject Matter Experts

Unfortunately, these *subject matter experts* are not marketers, writers, or salespeople. The tasks that make up their job description usually have very little to do with marketing, sales, or the lead funnel. However, to be successful, organizations must deliver this expert content to their buying audiences, and this only happens if subject matter experts can create it. It is unclear where this cost is incurred, because many subject matter experts who create content do so in an "extra-curricular" manner. Successful marketing organizations recognize this content gap and find ways to motivate, compensate, and encourage the creation of educational, Investigation-stage content by subject matter experts *and* to measure the cost to the organization that this content creation incurs. It can, however, be a difficult process.

MORE ACCURATE RESULTS

The way we measure our revenue process's effectiveness, results, and costs is changing because of the new ways we use to facilitate buyers in today's new revenue engines. To make the right decisions for allocating our investments, we must revisit our assumptions regarding the measurement of the cost of selling and marketing, what the correct measurements are, and how to test our campaigns. With this revised framework in place, we can better understand the overall effectiveness and efficiency of the revenue engine, and how we can best deploy our most valuable resources—in both marketing and sales—to increase our overall revenue results.

The next section looks at how to use this new understanding of buyers, our understanding of them, and the investments we make in facilitating their buying processes to see, benchmark, predict, and optimize our revenue-generation process.

Case Example

Realizing the depth and breadth of content consumed by the wide variety of buyers in the Platts buying process, the team shifted resources to ensure the needed content for the buyer's journey was created. Rather than focus on high level communications and events, the marketing team began to spend their time with product managers, commodities specialist, and domain experts. Learning everything they could about how each persona—analysts, traders, and executives—used the Platts products, they began to create deeper and richer content than ever before. This content then provided both the granularity of online behavior needed to detect buying signals, and the relevant topics needed to nurture interest over a long awareness stage prior to engaging with sales. This work to the form of persona profiles, case studies, and white papers.

PART

STOP <u>CRUNCHING</u> NUMBERS—START <u>CRUSHING</u> THEM

SEVEN

SEE: SUNLIGHT IS THE BEST DISINFECTANT

GAINING AN UNDERSTANDING OF YOUR REVENUE PERFORMANCE

For executives, the ability to understand and gain visibility into a corporate process is almost as valuable as any ability to make changes. Simply having that visibility enables us to effect change by asking the tough questions, highlighting metrics, or applying resources. The first step in the evolution from simply *crunching* numbers to *crushing* them is to gain a full understanding of your revenue engine's current performance.

A VIEW FROM ABOVE

If we think of the performance of the revenue engine as an end-to-end ecosystem, we can better understand the maximum potential for revenue performance, the areas that are candidates for optimization, and where performance is already well-optimized.

The highest dashboard view of the revenue engine highlights the entire revenue process—from your broadest market audience through the communication processes that influence their consideration of your solutions to the activities that shape final buying decisions.

Figure 7.1 – A View from Above

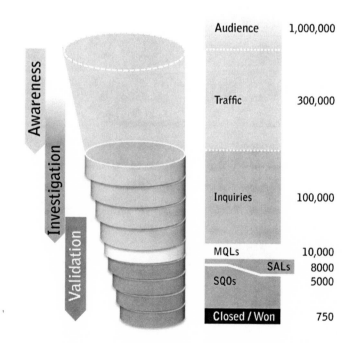

	Actual
Audience	1,000,000
Traffic	300,000
Inquiries	100,000
MQLs	10,000
SALs	8000
SQOs	5000
Closed / Won	750

Each element of this top-level view is comprised of the core metrics of a well-instrumented revenue process. The performance of each element in this view is guided by the underlying dynamics of how buyers interact with information and how they progress toward a purchase decision. Note, this is not a linear progression. This funnel view mainly provides insights into the shape and size of the revenue engine. However, we can only ascertain the health of each stage and the buyers' propensity to move forward after further investigation.

The following sections examine each stage in further detail and explore the best practices in building dashboards to show the current state of a revenue engine.

SHINING A LIGHT ON AWARENESS

At the Awareness stage, the revenue team focuses on getting messages and content to where the buyers are. For each market segment, there is a maximum potential audience that is either actively seeking information on options, open to learning more, or willing to be influenced by thought leaders. While we can expand this maximum audience in some instances through deliberate efforts, in many cases it is guided by market realities.

The goal of a high-performing revenue team is to maximize share of discovery within this maximum market audience. This metric shows how much of the conversation and awareness finds its way to your content, your solutions, and ultimately your products.

Naturally, it is challenging to track the progress of individuals at this stage of the process, so our measurements are ratios rather than conversion percentages. With an audience size of 1 million potential buyers, and 50,000 Web visitors linked to these sources of discovery, the share of discovery ratio is 5 percent. Increasing this percentage is crucial if you find you are not invited to compete in opportunities that appear to be ideal fits for your offerings.

RPM Dashboard—Share of Discovery

There are three primary avenues for buyers to become aware of your company and solutions: by actively seeking information (often via search), passively encountering information (often via ads), and being influenced to consider new information (often via social media). Executed properly, this awareness drives traffic to content on your website and requests for more information via Web form.

Each technique for generating awareness has a layer of deeper detail that indicates why it is or is not performing. But at the top level, we can simplify the performance metrics to audience, traffic, and inquiries. These metrics—across each method of discovery—provide insights into the issues that require investigation.

In each of the following examples, the net number of inquiries is increasing at a steady pace. However, this metric masks the underlying challenges that can only be seen with proper analysis.

The first example looks at active discovery. If the number of buyers actively seeking information on a solution category (the audience) is increasing, it likely reflects market interest that is moving in a positive direction. However, if the conversion rate for that audience's search interest is not translating into similar growth in traffic, it may indicate that you're not being discovered effectively. In this example, a strong upsurge in audience size masks the fact that the share of interest is dropping.

Figure 7.2 – **Share of Discovery – Active**

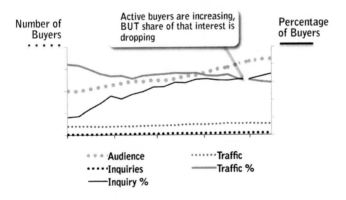

The second example looks at passive discovery. If advertising efforts reach a growing audience that passively becomes aware of your company and solutions, it will be reflected in traffic coming to your Web properties (assuming the conversion rate remains constant). However, if your ability to convert this traffic to any form of inquiry actually decreases, perhaps your content assets are losing their ability to entice prospective buyers to want to learn more. In this example, a strong upsurge in both audience size and resulting traffic masks a drop off in inquiry conversion rates.

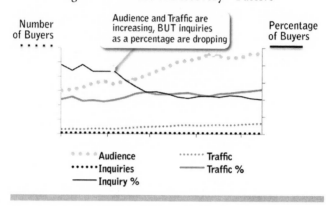

Figure 7.3 – **Share of Discovery – Passive**

A third example looks at influenced discovery. If your influence decreases with key opinion-makers, a simple tally of inquiry counts may obscure the underlying problem, especially if conversion rates are growing strongly due to excellent content. In this example, again, inquiry counts continue to grow, but are doing so because of great inquiry conversion. This masks the underlying problem that the audience being reached by influencers is dropping.

Figure 7.4 – **Share of Discovery – Influenced**

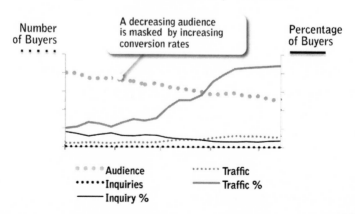

These top-level revenue performance management dashboards clearly show how prospective buyers are learning about your solution, how the trends are progressing, and whether you need to address any issues. Each area can be understood at a more detailed level through dashboards that provide insight into the internal mechanics of that area.

Active Discovery

One valuable area to understand is how your prospects actively discover your company and your solutions. The richness of the insights you can gain and the deep understanding of how buyers use search is virtually unparalleled. Each insight allows you to target your investments to maximize their effectiveness in driving your revenue performance.

Basics of Discovery

Let's first look at the 10 or 12 "main terms" that buyers most commonly associate with your solution category or industry. These are the primary search terms that, ideally, lead prospective buyers to your Web properties. To get a quick and solid idea of whether you're successfully being discovered, compare both the number of searches performed on each search phrase, and the number of visitors to your content based on those main terms. We can glean a few powerful insights that could inform our investment decisions:

- The number of searches is roughly the upper limit of what you can achieve with active awareness

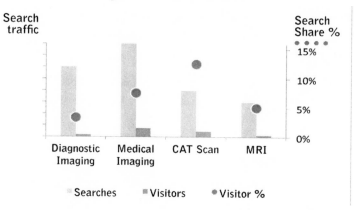

Figure 7.5 – **Share of Search**

efforts such as search engine marketing or search engine optimization. Broader awareness efforts such as analyst and public relations can also increase interest in your solution category.

- The number of visitors, and more importantly the percentage of visitors, who reach your site indicates how well your paid and organic search efforts are performing against each term. If a term is performing poorly, you might invest in search engine marketing for that term or focus on fresher content that improves your ability to be actively discovered by buyers.

This analysis also provides a good baseline of the total "audience" available in search. Leading search engines can provide the raw numbers of individuals who are searching for your main search terms (and any derivative search terms as well).

Deeper Searches

Remember, the way buyers seek information is changing. The average search phrase is now more than three words long, making it equally important to understand what is happening within the broader universe of search phrases used by buyers. The raw list of search phrases used by buyers to find you can be inherently informative. However, to more clearly understand the state of your revenue engine's performance, it's even more instructive to view the "longer tail" search phrases that prospects use. That gives you insight into their buyer stage.

To get a better sense of this metric, separate the searches that guide visitors to your website into four main categories:

- **Navigational**
  Searches that are simply a replacement for typing in your website URL, usually just your company name.

- **Main Terms**
  Searches for your main search terms for which you have deliberately optimized your site and marketing.

- **Long-Tail (Branded)**
  Deeper searches, often with multiple words in the search phrase, or searches for specific content that has your company or brand name in the phrase.

- **Long-Tail (Unbranded)**
  Deeper searches but without your company or
  brand name in the search phrase.

Figure 7.6 – **Search Categories**

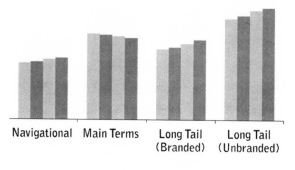

This dashboard shows how well your company and
solutions are being actively discovered. First, the relative
numbers of visitors who discover your offerings based
on long-tail phrases *vs.* main terms indicates whether
your content marketing strategies are effective. A greater
number of long-tail visitors likely indicates an effective
content marketing strategy. Since most searchers use
lengthy search phrases, if the long-tail columns are not
larger than the main term and navigational columns, it's
quite likely that your discoverability by buyers actively
seeking solutions is low. Consider investing in content
creation to have the long-tail content sought by buyers
available when they search.

Second, compare the volume of long-tail search phrases with and without your brand name (*i.e.* "high availability storage solutions" *vs.* "NetApp high availability storage products"). The use of your company name is a good indicator of whether buyers are in the Education stage (understanding the category) or are in the Investigation stage and are looking to learn more about your specific products.

Of course, overall trends are also very interesting. The effectiveness of natural search or your content marketing strategy grows slowly over time and its success is best observed by following the trends in these high-level numbers longitudinally.

Search Efficiency

To learn more from these views of your prospects' active discovery of your content, be sure to understand what traffic is driven by search engine marketing (SEM—paid

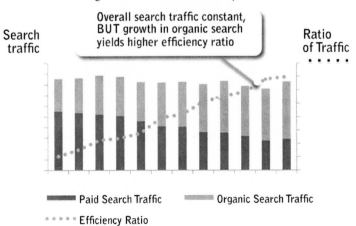

Figure 7.7 – Search Efficiency Ratio

ads placed beside search results) and what is driven by
search engine optimization (SEO—efforts to have content rank highly in natural search results)—and then improve your coordination and alignment of those initiatives. Most B2B marketing organizations invest in paid
search campaigns to drive awareness and most, if not all,
organizations can differentiate between traffic arriving
from paid search *vs.* natural search.

By segregating these two traffic sources and analyzing
their trends, we can learn more about the performance
of two very different marketing investments. Paid search
is predominantly a financial investment, and the results
are generally proportionate to the amount invested
(with reasonable fluctuations based on the skills of the
search engine marketing team and other variables, of
course). For this reason, you should expect the trend of
visitors from paid search to correspond to your SEM
investments.

Organic search efforts, however, are very different. The
investment here is primarily the time you spend creating
and promoting great content. Results build slowly as you
gradually gain credibility with search engines and key
influencers in the industry. Consistent, meaningful SEO
investments, therefore, result in a slowly but steadily
growing number of visitors driven by organic search
results.

This is why it's essential to *blend* these investments. SEM
investments can be made in areas that are new, where

results are weak, or where a short-term boost is needed. Investments in content and influence to drive organic search results can be done over time to achieve a longer-term, more sustainable impact. Measure the ratio of organic traffic to paid traffic to get an indicator of the efficiency of your overall efforts.

Measuring Discoverability

True success accrues to marketers whose content is discoverable by buyers as they seek information on their own. The most obvious component of this discover-ability is natural search. If a prospect searches for terms related to your business or the pains you solve, you want them to discover your organization. Early in the buy-ing process, you want them to discover your thought-leadership content and recognize you as a leader in the field. Later, in the Investigation or Validation phases, you want prospects to discover content that clarifies how to think about important aspects of the buying decision.

It's challenging, however, to measure this discoverability because there are an almost limitless number of search phrases that might be relevant to you and your solution. For each phrase, your main Web site, your social media properties—and competitor's Web properties may be discoverable. The best way to drive results is to have your content at or near the top of the search results for any relevant search phrases.

First, list the search phrases that are relevant to your solution. For each phase of the buying funnel, you will

Figure 7.8 – Discoverability Profile

Site	Top 1	Top 3	Top 10	Top 30	Top 100	Total
Yoursite.com	3	5	8	12	15	43
Yourblog.com	1	4	7	6	12	30
CompetitorA.com	12	15	23	34	14	98
CompetitorABlog.com	5	8	7	15	12	47
CompetitorB.com	1	1	3	2	5	12

■ Highest score

want to be found using a *different* set of phrases that vary based on the marketing challenge you face. For example, if your main challenge is a Flying Car challenge (buyers are unaware that your solution category even exists), you might primarily focus on the Awareness stage and come up with search phrases that are related to, but not identical to, your solution. If prospective buyers are unaware of your solution category, they may look for related or similar categories. Make sure you're discoverable there, too.

For each stage of the buying funnel, list the key phrases that buyers actively look for. At the Investigation phase, prospective buyers search for more precise category names. At the Validation phase, searchers may use your product name, even as they look for specific capabilities or objections.

Next, determine where your Web and social media properties (and your competitors') rank against those key phrases. One simple way to present this is a table showing your best ranking against each phrase summarized by how high each result ranks in the search engine results. Be sure to include search phrases where you would ideally be found, but currently are not.

On the left side, list your Web properties (both your main Web properties and social media properties). For comparison, also place your key competitors' Web properties on the left side of the chart. Along the top row, create columns for each of the following: First place, Top 3, Top 5, Top 10, Top 30, and Top 100. Then, for each search phrase, give each property a point in the highest ranking category it is discovered in.

For example, if "widget transportation" is a search phrase of interest, and your website appears as number 8 on the natural ranks on Google or Bing for that page, you would give yourself one point in the "top 10" category for your main website.

Complete this process for your top search phrases (around 100 phrases is a good number), and you will have a simple but very revealing discoverability profile for you and your competitors. Note that the first page of search results is generally considered the only page that matters in terms of traffic. Any results that are lower than the first page (top 10) are merely indications of progress, at best—they are unlikely to drive traffic.

Also note that results vary by search engine, geography, and over time. This report doesn't give a definitive answer, but it is a useful snapshot of whether you are making progress in becoming more discoverable.

Other Search Mediums

While any good marketer focuses on the "search majors" such as Google and Bing, be aware of the active discovery that takes place in other ways. Many social networks and content-sharing sites such as Twitter and YouTube have active discovery of information as a common usage profile. Whether it's one-time searches for specific information or continual searches that present the latest information on a particular topic, these are used by many people to receive relevant content.

While the importance of having a broad selection of shared content is also very relevant in these sites, each site has nuances in the way it allows users to discover information. Real-time sites like Twitter may use recency as a critical factor. Other sites prioritize information that comes from within your social network. Regardless of the nuances, if there is a significant audience of potential buyers who are actively seeking information in a medium other than Google or Bing, you need to ensure they can find your content, through whatever search means that platform offers.

Today, of course, the evolution of the social space is quite fluid and difficult to predict. While Twitter, Facebook, and YouTube may or may not be the relevant names a few years from now, the concept remains valid. For astute, revenue-focused marketers, any audience that actively seeks information on a relevant topic is often worth the investment to ensure that relevant, interesting content finds its way to that audience.

Passive Discovery

Understanding how your messages are passively discovered is an interesting factor in determining your investment strategy. Many paid techniques for passive discovery—such as banner advertising, for instance—are inherently trackable. However, it's equally true that the great content that allows your organization to earn passive discovery is often much less trackable.

First, compare paid *vs.* earned awareness. This metric gives you a clear sense of whether early-stage prospects are learning about you through paid efforts (e.g. advertisements) or through your efforts to earn their attention through content marketing. To create this comparison, chart the traffic to your website according to its originating source. Those who arrive from content sites or without any tracking codes are most likely those you've earned through your content marketing. Those who arrive with tracking codes from your online advertising are paid discovery efforts bearing fruit.

When we chart these two sources of awareness, we must first remove all active discovery (such as referrals from search sites such as Google and Bing) and all natural traffic (visitors who directly type in the URL without a referral). Also exclude "internal" sources of traffic, such as customer communities or online help portals because these individuals are already aware of you. This leaves just the visitors who discover your content, and hence become aware of your solutions, through either paid or earned awareness efforts.

Figure 7.9 – **Paid** *vs.* **Earned Awareness**

This view is instructive in two ways. First, a direct comparison of your paid and earned efforts shows whether latent opportunities exist. If you notice that prospects discover your solutions mainly from paid sources, you might assess whether content marketing efforts could be more economically efficient. If, however, all of your discovery traffic is coming from earned sources, you could consider refining your paid awareness efforts or increasing your paid awareness efforts to generate awareness in underserved areas of the market.

The second area of value from this view is visibility into how your efforts are creating more awareness over time. This is most crucial for earned media, which follows a "flywheel" dynamic for growth, whereby efforts to create and promote great content result in a slow and steady growth in awareness—much like a heavy flywheel spinning incrementally faster with each push that is applied. This dynamic is much different than the "lightning strike" of most paid media efforts where investments generate near-real-time results.

Calculating the total audience exposed to your messages for passive discovery is simple for paid audiences—it's usually a metrics provided by most ad platforms. But it's a different story with earned audiences. For paid audiences, the total coverage of your advertisements (number of "eyeballs") is a good audience proxy. However, when calculating the total audience for earned awareness (mostly in the form of content sites that mention your company or solutions), it may be simpler to assume a known conversion rate and use that to calculate the overall audience based on traffic.

While this technique obviously prevents any potential insights gained by understanding and analyzing traffic conversion rates, in earned passive awareness, this is often not something that can be easily optimized because there is such limited control over how and where you are mentioned. The best action is often simply to drive audience sizes higher by garnering more share of the conversation.

Analyzing Paid Discovery—Advertising and Audience Definitions

To show the effectiveness of advertising efforts, we focus on targeting audiences that will effectively convert into interested buyers. This area is evolving rapidly, and an important development lies in how we define audiences. Historically, an audience was defined mainly by the content itself, with a thin layer of demographics on top. For example, we used to be able to assume that an industry news site focused on printing technologies in

Figure 7.10 – **Analyzing Advertising Campaigns**

Audience	Audience impressions	Traffic		Inquiries		MQLs	
		#	%	#	%	#	%
Medical Diagnostics News	100,000	2000	2.0%	110	6%	8	7%
Imaging Technologies Site	80,000	1800	2.3%	140	8%	13	9%
Remarketing: High Lead Score	3000	450	15.0%	80	18%	10	13%
Remarketing: Recycled Opp	2000	180	9.0%	35	19%	12	34%

■ Highest score

Audiences defined by buying process stage via remarketing are smaller but more effective

the publishing sector had an audience of people involved in that discipline. Within this audience, advertisers often targeted by title or organization fit based on declared demographics, but not much more.

In today's online world, that whole context is rapidly changing. Major content networks are starting to enable advertisers to target audiences based on historical activity. For example, those who visit certain pages on your site, or meet certain qualification criteria could be defined as a specific audience, regardless of where they are on the Internet, and receive specific ads.

For advertising campaigns, this audience analysis becomes critical. While remarketing audiences are likely to be substantially smaller than their mainstream counterparts, they may convert into MQLs at a much higher rate or present more precise information that is relevant to latter stage Investigation and Validation only.

Inbound Links—Earning the Potential to be Discovered

Traffic coming to your Web properties is the most structured and visible metric when we analyze passive discovery. However, when it comes to earning this discovery, it is a suboptimal metric to guide decisions because it is an aggregate measure of all content that is linked to. Efforts to build great content and share it with influencers lead to a more measurable metric of inbound links.

An inbound link from another website to a page of your content is very valuable, both in terms of the new traffic it draws in and in the effect on search ranking. By creating interesting, useful, and valuable content, we can generate more of these links, each of which increases the chances that your content is discovered by prospects reading about the market space. Obviously, links from sites with greater traffic and credibility are more powerful and valuable than links from less relevant sites.

To measure the success of your content marketing strategy and identify areas for improvement, let's create

Figure 7.11 – **Inbound Links and the Potential to be Discovered**

Website	Total links	Avg. link quality	Visits	Inquiries
www.acme.com	120	34	1100	80
blog.acme.com	390	75	3600	430
mastersseries.acme.com	80	43	2600	190
webinars.acme.com	50	31	1900	210

Highest score

a dashboard of inbound links. For each major area of your Web properties, such as your main site, blogs, and campaign-specific sites, we'll list the total number of inbound links, the average quality for each inbound link (based on the traffic and credibility of the page the link resides on), and the number of visits generated by that link.

This dashboard view shows the effectiveness of your efforts to create exceptional content that inspires others to link to it. If top-level analysis of passive discovery shows levels of performance that are less than expected, an inbound link analysis can identify where the issues might be occurring.

Social Engagement and Passive Discovery

As social networks grow in importance for sharing and communicating information, they also gain a higher profile as the place where prospective buyers can get relevant information about new solutions and new approaches. Each conversation or engagement in this public domain—whether it's a LinkedIn discussion, an interaction on Twitter, or a question asked on Quora—creates an opportunity for another viewer to see the discussion and engage. While measurements in this area are evolving rapidly, it's valuable to have even a simple view of which social networks have a large number of links to your content, the total traffic to your content driven by each of these networks, and whether this traffic successfully converts into inquiries.

Figure 7.12 – Social Engagement and Passive Discovery

Social network	Shared links	Visits	Inquiries
Facebook	240	1200	95
Twitter	1230	4800	510
LinkedIn	320	2100	220

■ Highest score

Influenced Discovery

The current state of active and passive discovery can be assessed in a somewhat objective fashion—within limits. However, the third category—influence—is more difficult to measure because there is no definitive metric for measuring how much attention and influence each market influencer garners. Similarly, there is no easy metric showing how much mindshare you have with each individual influencer.

Unsurprisingly, however, technology in this space is moving at a rapid pace. The important concepts should be looked at and understood regardless of whether the data is captured manually, automatically, or through a combination of both techniques.

Internal Champions

As market influencers increasingly splinter into a larger number of smaller influencers, the importance of key internal contributors and personalities across all areas of your company cannot be underestimated. Each

> **Case Example**
>
> When launching a new product, a SOA layer for data services, that provided an advanced technical solution to a challenging problem, Informatica considered using a typical campaign structure of acquiring a large list and directly targeting that list with a promotion. However, based on their understanding of how their buyers sought information, Informatica took a different strategy. Starting a LinkedIn group on SOA-based data services, they invited top experts, a number of key customers, and relevant market influencers to join. By seeding the early discussions and contributing deep expertise to the conversations that were taking place, Informatica built a thriving community discussion. While entirely non-promotional in nature, the discussions were all centered around a topic area that Informatica had deep product capabilities in, and participants in the discussions quickly became aware of that set of solution capabilities.

individual brings an authentic personality, a unique perspective, and the capability to develop relationships with key external influencers in the market. This is *not* a capability that can be effectively provided solely by a marketing team, or an outsourced agency relationship.

Measuring the involvement of these internal champions is the only way to understand where you are with respect to developing a broad team of individuals who build relationships and "influence the influencers." Since these relationships guide market influencers, the individual champions form a crucial conduit to guiding and growing influence.

Key Influencers

To create a successful influence-based strategy, we must first get a complete handle on the universe of influencers. Identifying and measuring the potential reach of all of the influencers (content creators, bloggers, social influencers) is significantly more difficult than in previous years when only a small number of major influencers (key analysts and journalists) dominated the landscape. Now, with significantly more, but substantially smaller influencers in the market, it's far more challenging to understand their ability to reach an audience and get your messaging discovered.

Since these people are influencers, *not* a media channel, the message you relay through them is *not* under your control. Each influencer may understand, believe, and highlight different aspects of your message. Measuring this sentiment is important to understand their disposition toward you and your solutions. To begin to understand the influencer landscape, the following metrics are useful:

- **Community Size**
  The raw size of each influencer's potential community is generally the easiest to discover. Follower, friend, and connection counts in the various social networks are usually publicly available. If there is any newsletter or regular communication, they may be happy to share approximate list sizes, and blog subscriber counts for blogs with significant followers are often shared. Technologies such as PostRank

can show both the natural audience of a publisher's community, and how broadly shared that content is with a wider audience. We can safely assume that this area will continue to develop an ability to measure overall community size and breadth of sharing.

- **Influence Quality**

  A far more difficult metric to understand is *influence quality*—the likelihood that a member of the influencer's community is actually paying any attention. Technology here is evolving quickly, too. Products, such as Klout, approximate influence by analyzing sharing activities and conversation threads. It's still too early to determine who the technology leaders will be, but it is clear that estimates of influence within a particular topic area can be readily determined. Comparing each publisher's score against the score of the most influential publisher in the space provides an influence percentage that measures the publisher's relative influence within that space.

- **Mentions**

  Determine how frequently the influencer mentions your company or solutions to see how effectively they steer the market toward you. Counts of mentions in online articles and social media conversations give you a sense of this volume. Combine this with an analysis of sentiment to get a strong indication of whether the influencer is a positive advocate, neutral, or a detractor. Only view mentions in terms of a trend, because different publications have different propensities to mention specific solution names. On a per-publisher basis, calculate how frequently your name is mentioned as a percentage of the times when any competitive name is mentioned. This shows your share of awareness in this influencer's audience.

Together, these metrics provide an effective approximation of each influencer's audience size and your share of the conversation. Expanding this audience size by building stronger relationships with those influencers can create significantly larger opportunities to influence the thinking of a broader audience of prospective buyers.

Measuring Relationships

Once we identify the market's key influencers and your internal champions, we can create a dashboard to see how well you are developing the personal relationships that positively guide these influencers. Once again, this

Figure 7.13 – Influencer Audience Dashboard

Publication	Community raw size	Influence quality	Mention share	Influenced audience
Medical Device News	35,000	78%	60%	16,380
MediBlog	83,000	23%	10%	1909
Medical Tech Review	120,000	12%	25%	3600
Doctors Tech Blog	35,000	87%	60%	18,270

■ Highest score

Smallest community, BUT largest influenced audience

is a difficult concept to measure, but a good framework provides visibility into gaps, overlaps, and direction of progress.

- **Relationship Activity**
  For each influencer, track relationship activities to get a sense of whether your team is properly engaged with the influencer. Since most, if not all, influencers are online writers, you can track this activity very objectively. Each blog comment, each Twitter conversation, each LinkedIn discussion that your team has with an influencer is a relationship activity. Each is an opportunity to build awareness, convey messages, introduce new perspectives, or develop a deeper level of trust. While activity is only one aspect of a relationship, it's an important metric to track this across your entire team including subject matter experts.

- **Relationship Strength**
  For each relationship, ask each internal champion to use a scale of 1 to 3 to subjectively assess the strength of the relationship.

- **Sentiment**
  Mentions are usually only beneficial if they are neutral or positive and highlight your reputational/brand strengths, key differentiators, or your market perspectives. Track this for each influencer to understand whether they view your solutions favorably. Although "sentiment analysis" solutions are

evolving, the low volumes of mentions in a B2B environment, combined with the nuanced nature of identifying sentiment makes it likely that subjective analysis is your best option for the coming few years.

With each dimension analyzed, either objectively through appropriate technology, or subjectively with some manual work, you can gather a picture of how well your team is influencing the key influencers in your market. Over time, these relationships will develop and become an extremely effective way for your messages to reach your intended audience.

In this influencer dashboard, you can see that publications with the largest influenced audiences are ones where the relationship is weak and the sentiment is negative. At the same time, relationships with less-influential publications are being developed through many relationship activities.

Figure 7.14 – Influencer Management Dashboard

Publication	Influenced Audience	Relationship Activities	Relationship Strength	Sentiment
Medical Device News	16,380	2	☆	☹
MediBlog	1909	18	☆☆	☺☺☺
Medical Tech Review	3600	20	☆☆☆	☺☺
Doctors Tech Blog	18,270	0	☆	☹☹

■ Highest score

Largest influenced audience, yet little engagement

Internal Experts as Market Influencers

While the focus on building relationships with key market influencers should not be minimized, there is also an opportunity for key internal subject matter experts to become market influencers in their own right. The shift in the dynamics of how information is published has led to a movement from there being a small number of key influencers in any given market space (often analysts or journalists) to a larger number of smaller influencers (often bloggers or practitioners).

With this dynamic, there is an opportunity to directly influence markets by supporting or investing in internal experts to generate content, share opinions, and develop a personal brand. As they do so, their ability to influence markets through sharing selected views and framing discussions in the right light increases.

Converting Interest to Inquiry

Awareness efforts first generate Web traffic, an important step that educates the prospective buyer. But they don't initiate or foster a longer-term relationship. For that, the prospective buyer must first engage with the vendor, often by completing a Web form requesting a particular asset. But that information asset must have sufficient value that the prospect is willing to make the effort to request it.

To understand how various content assets perform against this challenge, let's create a dashboard to categorize content assets and chart their performance. For each content type, the average traffic to the landing page for the asset shows how much interest it is generating, while the average number of fields in the form is a proxy for the "inquiry barrier" presented to the prospect. The conversion percentage is the percentage of landing-page viewers who take the subsequent step of completing the request for the asset.

The following chart shows that the recorded demo and whitepaper assets have a low conversion rate, while the webinar and survey results are performing well. This may reflect on either the complexity of the form being used to gate the assets, or the perceived value of the assets themselves.

Figure 7.15 – **Asset Conversion Performance**

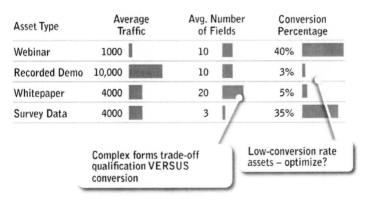

Asset Type	Average Traffic	Avg. Number of Fields	Conversion Percentage
Webinar	1000	10	40%
Recorded Demo	10,000	10	3%
Whitepaper	4000	20	5%
Survey Data	4000	3	35%

Complex forms trade-off qualification VERSUS conversion

Low-conversion rate assets – optimize?

In most cases, low conversion percentages either indicate an asset type that is not of high enough value or a Web form that is too daunting to complete. In either case, simple experimentation will show how best to optimize the content assets to maximize traffic conversion.

Inquiries and the Marketing Database

Awareness efforts focus on generating traffic and inquiries. However, in and of themselves, inquiries are merely requests for a marketing asset, registrations for an event, trials, or online demos. One individual prospect might submit multiple inquiries for various assets throughout this process. That buyer can only be understood if these separate inquiries and all other online actions are viewed and understood through a common lens.

To guide buyers through their Investigation stage and determine when they might be ready to engage with sales, we must recognize the actions of each buyer in total. To do this, as we discussed in Chapter 5, we need a marketing database to keep a clean, non-duplicated, and consistent view of each contact. While measurements of the Awareness stage end when the prospect makes an inquiry, subsequent measurements look at each buyer as an individual who may take many actions before a purchase.

Similarly, the marketing database is the foundation for a long-term relationship with prospects who may purchase a year or more in the future. Accordingly, the size and quality of the marketing database must be measured independently of the number of inquiries that are generated in a given quarter. Each new-name inquiry expands the database, and each existing-name inquiry indicates increased interest. Most buyers perform 10-20 inquiries in a buying process of any significant length.

ILLUMINATING YOUR DATA

To uncover how buyers progress through to the latter stages of investigation and validation let's first look at the marketing database that forms a foundation for this relationship. Now that we understand the Awareness stage better thanks to some high-level and detailed dashboards that showcase its performance, we can understand where inquiries are driven from. However, to guide those early-stage inquiries all the way to MQL status requires careful nurturing over a lengthy period of time. That's why high-quality, consistent data—and a clear understanding of that data—is crucial. This is the foundation for all other building blocks. A clear understanding means analyzing a number of important views: growth, activity, completeness, consistency, accuracy, and segment quality.

Growth and Total Size

The simplest two metrics—size of your database and its growth over time—show your marketing database's raw volume. Net new contacts add to your total, while bounce-backs and unsubscribes subtract from it. For this metric, be sure you are truly measuring *unique* contacts, without duplicates. The database should grow in a healthy manner, although growth rates can vary depending on your company and industry.

Active/Inactive

Equally important: what percentage of your database is active or inactive. Definitions can vary, but, for example, a minimum of three e-mails opened or clicked, one visit to the website, or one form submitted within a six-month time period can be an objective definition of an active prospect. Those who are inactive may have "emotionally unsubscribed," and are unlikely to become buyers. It's more important for the active component of your database to enjoy long-term growth than it is for your overall database to grow.

This simplified view of buyer engagement can detect some masked problems. In many organizations, the total database size may grow at a healthy rate, but most growth is in inactive contacts due to disengagement. In fact, in many cases, the number of active contacts may be shrinking over time, indicating a significant problem with the audience's willingness to engage with messaging.

Completeness

Analyze each important contact field for its completeness. In many marketing databases, many key fields are only 30 percent complete (or less), making it very difficult to use those fields for marketing efforts. If your fields are less complete than ideal, use progressive profiling (the technique of sequentially asking for small amounts of additional information from one buyer on separate visits, rather than a large number of questions at once) to add data to those sparsely populated fields.

Consistency

Even if a field is filled, it can be very difficult to derive value from it if the data is inconsistent (such as using "US", "U.S.", "USA" or "United States" to represent the same country). Fields like *Title, Industry, Country, State,* or *Revenue* are often extremely inconsistent as the data can be input in a wide variety of ways. Analyze each field to determine what values are in that field and their percentages to see if the data is generally consistent or inconsistent.

A reliable way to determine consistency is to total up the percentage of contacts whose values for a field fall within the most common 50 values for that field. A well-normalized and consistent field will likely have less than 50 "standard" values, so the percentage of contacts whose value for this field (such as industry) fits the normalized value will approach 100 percent. Conversely, fields such as e-mail address are not fit to be normalized, so will show almost 0 percent consistency.

In the chart, we can see that, although all fields are well completed, there is low consistency in the Industry and Title fields. This will result in challenges in building rules, segments, or analysis against the values in those fields.

Accuracy

A more difficult metric to assess is the accuracy of the data in the fields. This must be addressed on a

Figure 7.16 – Database Completeness and Consistency

Field	Completeness	Consistency (% in 50 most common)
Email Address	100%	0%
First Name	100%	5%
Last Name	100%	5%
Industry	95%	15%
Title	95%	10%
Revenue Range	80%	80%
Country	80%	80%
State/Province	80%	60%

■ Well normalized (>50%)
▨ Poorly normalized
□ n/a

! Fields such as Industry and Title should be normalized to increase qualification of database

field-by-field basis, usually with the assistance of third-party tools. Address validation services can assess or correct address information, tools to identify "aaaa" or "mickey mouse" as names can clear up contact information, and data-append services can assess or correct industry and revenue information by company.

Segment Quality

With a database that's complete, consistent, and accurate, you can assess whether you have the right individuals in your database. If your ideal buyer is a vice president of operations, and the geography you sell to is only continental Europe, you'll want to assess the number of names in your database that meet these criteria. If the size of this segment is insufficient to generate the needed business, you must begin marketing efforts targeting the very top of the revenue funnel.

Now that we have a handle on the quality, size, growth, and activity of your marketing database, we can examine the foundations of your ability to communicate with, and understand, your buying audience. Now, it's possible to analyze your overall revenue process.

WATCHING LEAD MATURATION

The lead-management process can last for months, if not years. You nurture prospective buyers, keeping them engaged and educated. You present ideas, discuss opportunities, and respond to objections through events, webinars, socially shared content, and other means. While many diverse activities are underway during this stage, we can create dashboards to capture the important trends and themes, and guide behavior.

Creating Qualified Leads

The marketing core of the revenue engine is where buyers are nurtured—from initial contact until a buying process is identified and the prospect is handed off to the appropriate sales resource. As we discussed earlier, although we often visually represent this process as a funnel, it does not mean that buyers progress in a linear path through this phase. Their progress is guided more by internal dynamics within their organizations than by a vendor's marketing or sales teams.

At a high level, we can build a dashboard view of this stage that presents the most important information regarding the size, shape, and velocity of leads in the

Figure 7.17– **Creating Qualified Leads**

Revenue Funnel		Q1	Q2	
		Actual	Actual	Growth % (Actual)
Total Names		100,000	110,000	10%
Names by Fit	D	25,000	27,500	10%
	C	25,000	27,500	10%
	B	25,000	27,500	10%
	A	25,000	27,500	10%
Names by Engagement	4	70,000	78,300	12%
	3	15,000	16,000	7%
	2	10,000	10,500	5%
	1	5000	5200	4%
Qualified Leads	A1	100	125	25%
	A2	100	125	25%
	B1	100	125	25%
	C1	100	125	25%
Total Qualified Leads	MQLs	400	500	25%

! Funnel growing, BUT
mainly unengaged buyers

revenue engine. The first view, essentially a snapshot of the marketing database, presents a point-in-time picture of the individuals within the marketing database. First, we can split this view along the dimensions of "fit" to show the size and shape of the funnel from the viewpoint of whether the prospects are likely to have long-term potential to purchase. Next, we can segment out this view according to "engagement" to get a view of the size and shape of the funnel based on the prospect's likelihood to be interested in a near-term purchase.

From this set of names, we draw the MQLs based on the combined criteria of fit and engagement that have been agreed upon by marketing and sales. The total MQLs created in a quarter shows the flow of new leads into the sales team.

Finally, we can create a view that shows progress over time by showing the same data on a quarter-by-quarter basis. This shows what has moved ahead based on the aggregate efforts of the revenue team. Watch for anomalous changes in the shape of the funnel: too few leads added to the top or too little activity indicative of near-term buying interest.

Buyers and the Content Matrix

Ultimately, however, what drives buyers through a buying process is content. It can be delivered or discovered in a multitude of ways, but without content that convinces, intrigues, explains, and excites, buyers are most unlikely to move forward with a buying effort. Each buying role has unique information needs and interests throughout the buying process, and that means marketing must focus on creating content to meet each role and need. Some needs are clearly defined and the information will be deliberately sought. For instance, a technical buyer might want to understand whether a key functional capability exists in your solution.

However, many other needs are neither clearly defined nor deliberately sought. These include perceptions and preconceived notions as well as education on important buying criteria to consider. For example, an economic

Case Example

The FifthThird bank team spoke with many of their customers and prospective customers, and realized that expectations for information had shifted dramatically. While a few years ago, information on the bank and its services would mainly have been exchanged through conversations with professional salespeople, prospective buyers now went online to seek that information. Realizing this, the FifthThird team undertook a comprehensive redesign of how they made information accessible. They defined a matrix of buyer personas, stages in the buying process, and information formats (such as podcasts, videos, and spec sheets) in order to map out the relevant information needs of their audience.

At each stage of the buying process, the content was designed to achieve a specific objective. In the awareness stage, the content was created to establish FifthThird's thought leadership and credibility. As the buyer progressed to the investigation stage, the content was designed to assist that buyer in establishing their own credibility within their organization for the solutions they were recommending. At the final stage of the buying process, validation-oriented content established the bank's track record, analyst ratings, and the profiles of the senior leadership team, assuring the buyer that they were making a safe decision.

Providing this information both in a resource center, and selectively placed throughout the FifthThird website at points where buyers would be most likely to discover it allowed the buyers to guide their own buying process both before their interaction with the sales team, and also during a sales engagement.

buyer might perceive that your solution is ill-suited for financial services organizations. Or a user buyer might not realize that having a routine task completed in one click rather than eight can have more effect on her user experience than any other feature.

It can be useful to audit your existing marketing content to understand what you currently have available and what new material is required. This audit lets you create a "content grid" that helps you define how you leverage your content in buyer education as well as your content development strategy. Creating the matrix is straight-forward. For each relevant buyer, list the key messages that must be understood by them to achieve a successful purchase. Some messages will be objections, others will be value propositions or benefits.

Next to each message, list the content assets that convey or support these messages. Then rank their effectiveness. The effectiveness metric depends on what medium the asset is being used in, or a blend if it us used in multiple. For example, if it is an e-mail campaign, an open or click-through rate would be an appropriate metric. If it's an advertisement or search ad, a click-through or in-quiry rate might be the right metric. Each metric should be normalized to the average for that media type to be somewhat comparable.

In the following grid, for example, we can see that we are likely doing a poor job communicating effectively about integration or the value of our community to technical buyers, while we are doing a great job communicating with user buyers about the courses available and our mobile capabilities.

Figure 7.18 – Content Effectiveness Matrix

Buyer	Message	Asset	Effectiveness	
Technical Buyer	Integration Value Proposition	Integration Whitepaper	10%	
	Technology Stack Objection	Analyst Technology Report	35%	
		Benchmark Performance Report	42%	
	Skill set Objection	Community Overview	12%	
		Industry Skill Landscape Report	65%	
User Buyer	Usability Benefits	Product Free Trial	36%	
		User Video Testimonial	27%	
	Mobile Application Benefits	Mobile Application Demo	52%	
	Training Objection	Course Overview	73%	
		User Video Testimonial	27%	
Economic Buyer	Total Cost of Ownership Advantage	ROI Calculator	16%	
	Community/Ecosystem Advantage	Community Overview	48%	
	Up-Front Cost Objection	Financing Options Document	43%	

> **!** Low effectiveness scores highlight content gaps

Now, you can quickly see which buyer types aren't being reached and which messages are not being effectively communicated. By identifying and quickly addressing content gaps, you can optimize the lead management stage of the revenue engine.

Content and the Publisher Mindset

The need for content, as we discussed in Chapter 2, is exponentially greater in today's buyer-controlled world than it was historically. This analysis of content gaps highlights this challenge by showing the content that buyers need to delve into your solution and assess its fitness for their business. This content must span a broad range of topic areas, at unprecedented levels of detail.

To achieve this content richness, marketers must adopt a publisher's mindset, a process that supports the steady creation of high-quality content on a variety of in-depth topics for a wide range of buyer roles and perspectives. The publisher mentality is much more appropriate for populating this type of content matrix than the outdated notion of the classic B2B marketer.

Content, Publishing, and the Ideal Frequency

It can be difficult to assess your audience's awareness of your company solutions and how actively your marketing efforts are securing or maintaining their awareness. However, we can measure how effective your marketing tactics are in building this awareness. Each tactic, whether it's an event, a webinar, a promotion, a whitepaper, or a research report, will be relevant to a certain segment of your marketing database. As you develop these marketing assets and communicate them to your audience, you must strike a careful balance between building awareness and over-communicating.

Create a high-level analysis of your communication patterns to identify any awareness gaps or over-communication risks. Since many, if not most, outbound communication touch points will be via e-mail, it is the e-mail frequency patterns that provide the best insight into your overall communication patterns. As we know, e-mail is not as "free" a medium as it appears. Only when permission costs are calculated can its true cost be seen.

To look at this, let's create a communication frequency spectrum by graphing the number of outbound (typically e-mail) touch points in a three-month period compared to the number of people who received that many messages. As this graph shows, you generally see a large number of people who receive zero, one, or two e-mails from you in the period, and a steady decline in people receiving more e-mails than that. This gives you a sense

Figure 7.19 – **Communication Frequency Spectrum**

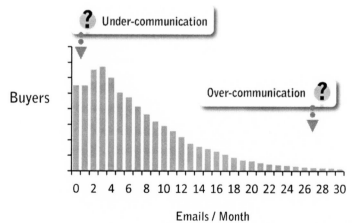

of high-level trends in outbound communication. Are there people who are not hearing from you at all—but should be? Are there people you are over-communicating with?

What is the Correct Frequency?

The question soon arises: is there an ideal frequency for communication for all recipients? Not at all. Highly engaged buyers, late in the buying process and involved in many events and webinars, expect frequent communications. However, early-stage prospects who are only casually keeping themselves educated on industry topics, neither want nor expect frequent communication. Creating the same frequency spectrum, but split by buyer engagement to show one spectrum each for buyers of high, medium, and low engagement can show where there is a mismatch of interest and communication that should be corrected.

The right content for each buyer, nurtured at the right frequency, forms a recipe for creating marketing qualified leads. When interest is detected, based on a visitor consuming certain content, we can assume the prospect is ready to engage and hand him off to the sales team.

The Marketing to Sales Hand-off and the Net Quality Score

While vitally important, the nurturing and discovery of qualified leads is of limited value unless we have a smooth and efficient hand-off of qualified leads to sales. Since this process involves a significant behavioral element in engaging the sales team, it can be the source of many easily remedied revenue engine challenges.

The first aspect is to assess the volume and quality of leads flowing into each territory. Volume is, of course, a simple metric to dashboard, and volume differences by territory can be quickly identified. Quality, however, is often a more important predictor of success. While MQLs may be defined as any lead that falls into a fit and engagement profile that defines it as an A1, A2, or B1, that doesn't mean all MQLs are equal. Understanding the quality of leads passing to each territory is vital to determine whether any revenue challenges are a result of poor team performance or poor lead quality.

> A useful metric here is the *Net Quality Score.* It indicates the overall balance of high- and low-quality leads being sent to each rep or territory. We calculate the Net Quality Score by sorting leads into high (*e.g.* A1), medium (*e.g.* A2.), and low (*e.g.* B1 and B2) categories. The Net Quality Score is the number of high-quality leads minus the number of low-quality leads, divided by the total number of leads. Scores can range from –100% to +100%, and higher scores indicate a higher average lead quality.

This quality score quickly pinpoints issues. For example, the following chart shows that, while the Central region is receiving a large number of leads, they are generally of very low quality. This may limit the sales team's performance and effectiveness through no fault of their own.

Figure 7.20 – Lead Hand-off and Net Quality Score

Territory	Rep	A1	A2	B1/B2	Total MQL	Net Quality Score	
East	Sally Jones	30	10	6	46	52%	
East	John Smith	20	8	11	39	23%	
West	Preeya Gupta	16	10	12	38	11%	
West	Neil Johansen	26	14	10	50	32%	
West	Bob Clark	122	50	51	203	32%	
West Total		164	74	73	311	29%	
Central	Andy Weston	10	20	140	170	-76%	
Central	Jane Chen	8	12	162	182	-85%	
Central Total		18	32	302	352	-81%	
Total		182	106	375	663	-29%	

High number of MQL, BUT very low quality

Now that we see which territories, product lines, and salespeople are receiving leads and what their quality is, our next step is to generate some insights into the outcome of those leads. The disposition of leads by a sales team after an initial contact attempt should yield some important insights into whether any fine-tuning of the qualification process is required. If the leads were unreachable, lacked interest, were not the right role, or only had early-stage interest, marketing can assess potential quality issues with their leads. Likewise, if certain sales reps are doing a poor job following up with quality leads, this also shows up in the analytics of lead disposition through an MQL-to-SQO conversion ratio for each salesperson.

In the following lead-disposition chart, for example, Bob, Andy, and Jane received a large number of leads, but failed to convert many to opportunities. Instead, they marked them as "unable to connect." Note, however, that the net number of opportunities created remains on par with the team because the poor conversion rate was masked by the high volume of leads.

Figure 7.21 – **Lead Disposition**

Rep	Total Leads	Did not Connect	Wrong Role	Call back in 90	No interest	Oppty Created	MQL/SQO Conversion Rate	
Sally Jones	46	12	8	8	10	8	17%	
John Smith	39	10	12	8	3	6	15%	
Susan Alston	51	22	12	5	3	9	18%	
Brianna Jones	66	10	18	11	10	17	26%	
Preeya Gupta	38	8	2	9	8	11	29%	
Neil Johansen	50	14	10	8	9	9	18%	
Bob Clark	203	140	11	26	18	8	4%	
Andy Weston	170	123	12	8	18	9	5%	
Jane Chen	182	138	5	25	5	9	5%	

❗ High number of leads, BUT very low conversion

This may be an indication of a performance or training challenge with these sales reps, or it could be that the volume of leads was so high that they were unable to truly dedicate sufficient effort to each lead.

LOOKING AT PIPELINE

When we examine the final stage of interaction with buyers—the sales pipeline—we can gain many insights regarding why prospects are buying—and why they are not. Each insight can translate into actions and investments in sales skills, selling process, content creation, or campaign strategy. There are three main aspects that merit our attention at this stage of buyer behavior: size, shape, and speed.

Size

The most obvious metric to examine is the *size* of the sales pipeline. In any given quarter, some opportunities will close. Sometimes prospects will select a competitor or decide on an alternate plan. And some opportunities remain viable but postpone to the next quarter. For this reason, most organizations must manage a pipeline that is three to six times the bookings quota for the quarter.

Figure 7.22– **Pipeline Size**

Closing			Q1	Actual	
			Opps	Pipeline ($K)	% of Pipeline
Sales Opportunities	e	Needs Analysis	800	$8,000	40%
	d	Solution Presentation	800	$8,000	40%
	c	Solution Proposal	200	$2,000	10%
	b	Commitment & Negotiation	200	$2,000	10%
Bookings	a	Closed Won	100	$1,000	
		Total Pipeline		$20,000	

Size, however, can be deceptive if we look at in isolation, because many actions and efforts contribute to the size of a revenue pipeline, including the decisions of individual sales reps. For this reason, if an executive wants to see a large pipeline, most sales teams will quickly show one. But this doesn't factor in the quality of the opportunities in that pipeline.

Shape

Just as important as the size of an overall pipeline is its *shape*. A healthy pipeline shows opportunities at all stages of the buying cycle and does not betray any tendency for opportunities to get "stuck" at a particular stage.

The validity of any pipeline shape is only as good as the analysis to determine if an opportunity belongs (and, if time has passed, still belongs) at a certain stage. Reaching this determination based on sales activity, prospect

Figure 7.23 – **Pipeline Shape**

Sales Stage	Current Quarter Actual		This Time Last Quarter		Shape Variance	
	Opps	Pipeline ($K)	Opps	Pipeline ($K)	Opps	Pipeline ($K)
e Needs Analysis	1000	$9,500	800	$8,000	25%	19%
d Solution Presentation	750	$7,000	600	$6,000	25%	17%
c Solution Proposal	300	$3,600	400	$4,000	-25%	-10%
b Commitment & Negotiation	100	$1,250	200	$2,000	-50%	-38%
a Closed Won	100	$1,000	100	$1,000	0%	0%
Total Pipeline	2,150	$21,350	2,000	$20,000	8%	7%

! Pipeline has increased, BUT shape has worsened

activity, and customer-based verifiable outcomes is critical in maintaining a pipeline shape that is accurate and objective.

In many businesses, especially in the technology field, there's a strong tendency for most deals to happen toward the very end of the quarter. If this is the case, one key metric of pipeline health is *Shape Variance*—the comparison of the current pipeline shape to the same point in the previous quarter (or the same period a year ago). This snapshot shows whether today's shape changes are the result of natural variance throughout a quarter, or arising from an important underlying change in buyer dynamics or sales performance.

This chart shows a pipeline that appears to be growing overall, but on closer examination, a significant decrease in deals at the Commitment and Negotiation stage, compared to last quarter may indicate a problem.

A well-managed pipeline shape shows a well-run revenue-generating team that maintains an appropriate balance between closing deals for the current quarter and developing new opportunities in the pipeline that will close in future quarters. Variances in the size and shape of a pipeline are natural throughout a quarter—and to be expected. However, analyzing pipeline shape over a longer period of time can yield interesting insights regarding both sales team performance and the ability of the marketing team to contribute qualified leads to the pipeline.

Figure 7.24 – **Pipeline Shape and the Front-End Load Ratio**

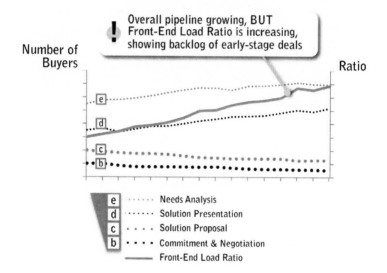

A measurement of this overall pipeline shape, called the front-end load ratio, can be instructive. Early-stage deals—such as E (Needs Analysis) and D (Solution Presentation)—can be characterized as in the front end of the sales process. Meanwhile, deals in the late stages— such as C (Solution Proposal) and B (Commitment and Negotiation)—should be considered to be in the back end of the sales process.

The ratio between these two sums—front-end deals divided by back-end deals—gives an indication of the overall shape of the pipeline. An increase in the front-end load ratio shows that the pipeline is increasingly front-end loaded. While its overall size may remain large, a near-term revenue challenge may lurk.

Speed

Perhaps the most underappreciated metric in analyzing the sales end of the revenue pipeline is *speed*—for two reasons. First, the impact of speed is identical to the impact of pipeline size, all other factors being equal. Reducing the average time-to-close by 50 percent has the same impact on revenue as doubling the overall size of the pipeline.

Second, the value of speed in understanding deal dynamics and challenges is without parallel, providing far more insight into optimization opportunities than size alone. If a spate of "stuck opportunities" appears, it can often lend crucial insights into objections, gaps in communication, or messaging that fails to connect with buyers. Without careful and precise tracking of pipeline speed, these insights do not surface.

Days Leads Outstanding: A Measure of Speed

The best way to measure pipeline speed in a forward-looking manner is by measuring *days leads outstanding (DLOs)*. Using the defined criteria of a qualified lead, the measure of how long a lead has been in an active sales process is very relevant. Deals that successfully close generally move through the pipeline at a good pace. Deals that have stagnated in the pipeline longer than the average time to close merit a higher level of scrutiny. It's helpful to look at days leads outstanding by territory, and compare it to both the average DLO for deals that close and the timeframe under which 80 percent of deals

Figure 7.25 – Days Leads Outstanding

close (to eliminate outliers). This gives us a quick view of where the pipeline bottleneck is and shows where further investigation and optimization are needed.

Size, Age, and the Pipeline Speed Ratio

As we showed earlier, the pipeline dimensions of size and speed are, in many ways, interrelated. A larger pipeline with the same speed has the same effect on net revenue as a faster pipeline with the same overall size. However, this interrelationship can mask pipeline problems. If the average deal size within the pipeline shrinks, while the average age of the pipeline increases, the overall size will appear constant—yet significant problems are obviously present beneath the surface.

To observe this dynamic and spot revenue problems before they become significant, a dashboard view of the *pipeline speed ratio* is valuable. This speed ratio is the average deal size divided by average age (measured in

Figure 7.27 – **Pipeline Speed Ratio**

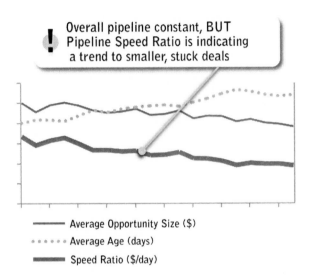

$/ day). If this ratio is decreasing, it means that deals are shrinking while average age is increasing, indicating a significant revenue challenge—smaller, slower deals—lies ahead.

DASHBOARDING TO GUIDE BEHAVIOR

The dashboards in this section provide executive-level views of what's happening within the revenue engine and provide visibility into the process from early-stage awareness to the final closing. This gives us the opportunity to assess performance as well as record a baseline from which to optimize and increase that performance.

While providing that structure, however, dashboarding also provides an important behavioral guide.

Throughout the organization, the simple awareness that a set of metrics is being dashboarded and viewed by senior executives will inevitably shape behaviors and lead revenue teams to better decisions. Knowing the results of ineffective marketing campaigns, lackluster content, or poor sales execution will be seen and understood is a powerful motivator, and will change a team's behavior quickly.

After achieving the visibility that dashboards provide, however, our next step is to use these benchmarks to understand performance and areas of opportunity so that we can increase our focus on the areas that exhibit the greatest potential to impact and improve the performance of the revenue engine.

ONE

BENCHMARK: KNOW WHERE YOU STAND

UNDERSTAND YOUR AREAS FOR IMPROVEMENT

Visibility alone certainly helps motivate teams to move revenue performance in the right direction. However, an understanding of *where* to focus efforts can only be achieved with a view into strengths and weaknesses.

BENCHMARK OPTIONS

The art of revenue performance management is in continual improvement of all aspects of the revenue engine. To build a high-performance process, it must not only be instrumented and measured to give you transparency into its current state, it must also be continually improved. As the market, technologies, competitors, and your own capabilities change, you must continually adapt, learn, and optimize. To do that, you need to know where you are performing well in the overall revenue process and where you need to shore up your performance. That's where benchmarking enters the picture.

Revenue performance benchmarks can be designed in three main ways:

- against alternatives to ensure you use the most effective and efficient way to accomplish a tactical objective.

- against a plan to ensure each element of the revenue performance process contributes at the required level.

- against best-in-class standards to ensure your performance matches—or exceeds—top performers in your industry.

Against Alternatives

The best way to start benchmarking is to examine individual components of the revenue process and ensure that each element is performing as well as alternative options. To accomplish this, we must establish a clear comparison metric that can be seen as equivalent. If, for example, we're comparing a webinar and a whitepaper marketing campaign, they can only be reasonably compared with a clear definition of what the outputs should be.

If, for example, the immediate goal of the two marketing campaigns is to drive MQLs for sales, that metric is a fair comparison. Metrics such as website traffic and raw inquiries will be too high in the funnel to be meaningful, and metrics such as sales pipeline movement or closed business will be too disconnected from the initiative to be useful.

When you're benchmarking alternatives, you can only fairly compare initiatives that are truly alternatives to each other and that drive the same intended outcome. A humorous video that builds awareness cannot be reasonably compared to a webinar campaign that creates MQLs. And you can't fairly or plausibly compare it to an inside sales campaign that drives business to a close.

Against a Plan

Before we benchmark our efforts across the entire revenue process, we must first develop a comprehensive model of the entire end-to-end buying process and determine conversion metrics at each stage. Basing our plan on this model, the volumes, velocity, and conversion rates that we achieve can be compared to the planned rates, and we can make appropriate adjustments.

In building this plan, we often uncover key gaps in revenue performance, especially at transition points between siloed groups. By identifying these gaps, we can devise initiatives and investments to bring the conversion rates to reasonable levels and improve overall revenue performance.

The uniqueness of each business situation cannot be underestimated in creating this plan. Plan targets are often only viable in context of what has been achieved historically, so a solid planning exercise generally encompasses cycle of measuring past performance, extrapolating to the future, and selecting key areas to optimize.

Against Best in Class

Armed with a comprehensive view of revenue performance, we can now benchmark against best-in-class companies. Naturally, each business's experiences vary, but by benchmarking revenue-funnel metrics against best-in-class companies, it's easy to quickly spot potential areas of improvement.

Ideally, your benchmarks should stay within your industry vertical. That eliminates variability of buyer dynamics and allows insightful comparisons of funnel sizes, overall buying velocity, and conversion rates. Similarly, try to structure your comparisons to other organizations that share a similar go-to-market strategy (such as a free-trial program), or that pursue comparable deal sizes. This can yield valuable insights regarding conversion rates and response profiles.

Each style of benchmarking adds value in its own unique way, and the more visibility you gain into the performance of your revenue engine, the more you can make needed optimizations and improvements.

CHALLENGES IN BUILDING BENCHMARKS

As you design and craft the benchmarks to guide your revenue engine, a number of key challenges arise. Each can be overcome, but they are worth exploring in some depth, as they can lead to frustration if ignored.

The Changing Dimensions of Lead Flow

In building your end-to-end plan for managing revenue performance, stay aware of how the dimensions change over time. As you interact with a prospect, that prospect's defined characteristics change as you forge a more direct connection. While this change is unimportant if you deal with each stage separately, in the aggregate it can become important to understand and model correctly.

- At the earliest stages, as the prospect enters the Awareness and Education stage, we can track metrics concerning interactions and views. Whether it is views of a banner ad, anonymous visitors to a website, or searches of key phrases, these views are often anonymous and may occur multiple times for the same individual.

Figure 8.1 – **Changing Dimensions of Lead Flow**

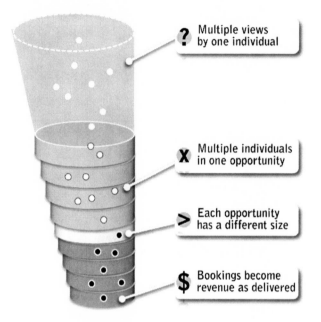

? Multiple views
by one individual

X Multiple individuals
in one opportunity

> Each opportunity
has a different size

$ Bookings become
revenue as delivered

- As individual prospects become known, uniquely identifying them through an e-mail address or other ID is possible. Now we can link multiple interactions with one person and that individual's actions can begin to qualify them as potentially being an MQL.

- As an MQL is handed off to the sales team, and sales creates an opportunity to explore the MQL's interest, the buyer's company usually has multiple stakeholders.

- We can start to "size" the opportunity itself as it is explored in further detail. This could be an annual contract value, total deal size, or other measurement of bookings.

- When a deal closes and services begin to be rendered, this bookings number translates into a flow of revenue based on the appropriate accounting standards being used.

At each milestone in the overall plan, these dimensions will shift. Generally, this does not present a problem and allows for no issues in planning. If, for example, 15 opportunities are created from 1,000 leads, a 1.5 percent conversion rate is a fine number to plan against. Similarly, if 15 opportunities leads to $300,000 in closed business, a revenue close rate of $20,000 per opportunity can form a good basis of a plan.

However, this assumes that no fundamental changes are happening. If the number of contacts per account in a given list is three times higher than your typical group of leads, this will directly affect the 1.5 percent conversion rate. Similarly, a marketing campaign that is targeted at an enterprise product set with a much higher average selling price, the ratio of $ closed to opportunities will no longer be valid.

Time and Measurement

Our benchmarking efforts must also carefully consider the effect of time. To understand true conversion rates between stages of the buying funnel, we must look carefully at how these conversion rates are measured. Marketing campaigns executed at one point in time will not

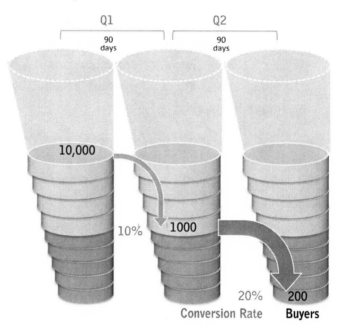

Figure 8.2 – **Conversion Ratios and Time**

have instantaneous effects. In fact, the distant effect on final revenue results may not materialize for months or quarters after the campaign.

In companies with high growth rates or shifting revenue engine models, a group of leads generated in Q1 may perform quite differently than leads generated in Q3— perhaps arising from changes in the marketing team, metrics, messaging, or market conditions. To correctly account for this, any measurement of conversion rates or results must take into account the expected amount of time required for a lead or MQL to complete a funnel stage.

If the average lead takes 90 days to move from Mildly Interested to MQL and the average time between MQL and Closed Won is also 90 days, then our measurement of close rates between Mildly Interested and Closed Won must compare deals closed in Q3 with Mildly Interested Leads from Q1. Without this correction for time, our conversion rates would not reflect the reality of how prospects buy and how long it takes for them to move through the buying process.

BENCHMARKING ALTERNATIVES

In the course of implementing your campaigns, you will need to make numerous decisions within the revenue engine that require a choice between two alternatives. Should we use paid search ads or banner ads to drive awareness? Would a tradeshow or a webinar series drive a greater number of qualified leads? Which members of the sales team close more business? Before comparing these alternatives, we must first understand how to best measure them.

Awareness—Comparing Paid Efforts

Effectiveness:

We can compare our pay-for-awareness efforts on two main dimensions: effectiveness and efficiency. Effectiveness is the ability to drive high-volume, high-quality awareness. We do this by comparing the effort to the key metrics of the Awareness stage: audience, traffic, and inquiries. Benchmarking awareness efforts on this basis

Figure 8.3 – Comparing Effectiveness of Paid Efforts

Campaign	Search - "Medical Devices" campaign	Search - "Imaging Systems" campaign	Ads - Webinar Banner	Ads - Demo Promotion
Audience	130000	210000	300000	120000
Traffic	1400	2500	1000	4200
Audience Conversion	1.1%	1.2%	0.3%	3.5%
Inquiries	250	340	230	180
Traffic Conversion	18%	14%	23%	4%
MQLs	19	27	24	15
Lead Conversion	8%	8%	10%	8%
Traffic to MQL Conversion	1.4%	1.1%	2.4%	0.4%

❗ Demo promotion drove more traffic BUT webinar banner resulted in more MQLs

is a fairly standard exercise, but top revenue teams often add *lead quality* to the mix to see if the interest they're generating is truly qualified. By tracking campaign performance through to MQL, a measure of quality is provided.

Many campaigns drive traffic and inquiries but deeper investigation can show that the quality of those inquiries might be substandard, implying that we should invest in other awareness campaign options.

The following chart shows that early metrics may be misleading. The ads for the demo promotion drove significant traffic, but it was unqualified traffic, as all other campaigns generated more MQLs, even with smaller traffic levels.

Efficiency:

While benchmarks of effectiveness show the success of our awareness campaigns, they do not show whether the campaigns drove those results efficiently. We need efficiency benchmarks to show the costs incurred in driving the results.

With paid awareness, most campaign costs are cash expenses, but there are also people and permission costs. With proper cost allocation, we can benchmark multiple

Figure 8.4 – **Comparing Efficiency of Paid Efforts**

Campaign	Search - "Medical Devices" campaign	Search - "Imaging Systems" campaign	Ads - Webinar Banner	Ads - Demo Promotion
Cost	$10,000	$15,000	$28,000	$14,000
Audience	130,000	210,000	300,000	120,000
Traffic	1400	2500	1000	4200
Cost per Visitor	$7.14	$6.00	$28.00	$3.33
Inquiries	250	340	230	180
Cost per Inquiry	$40.00	$44.12	$121.74	$77.78
MQLs	19	27	24	15
Cost per MQL	$526	$556	$1,167	$933

! Allocated against costs, however, the webinar is the **most expensive** MQL source

awareness efforts against each other. Much like the effectiveness benchmarks, the cost per MQL provides the best indication of which investments will drive revenue success.

With costs allocated against the same data from the previous chart, we can see that the cost per MQL varies widely: the webinar banner was the most expensive, and the search campaigns were the most cost-effective awareness effort.

Earned Awareness and the Flywheel Challenge

As we benchmark our numerous awareness-building efforts to properly assess their effectiveness, it's not uncommon to encounter what's called the "flywheel" dynamic. In a flywheel investment, efforts to increase awareness translate into an incremental increase in community size or engagement, but the community, once formed, remains a source of awareness among its members for an extended period of time.

To analyze investments that show a flywheel dynamic, it's often more meaningful to look at the effect that the investment had in terms of increasing the flywheel's speed, rather than looking at immediate effects on buyers.

We typically see the flywheel dynamic in awareness efforts that focus on social media or community building. Since success is mainly defined by the size and quality of a community you attract and engage, the efforts can exhibit a flywheel dynamic. Let's compare a content-creation effort on a blog with a similar initiative on Facebook. The relevant metric is the change in community size arising from each initiative. If blog subscribers increase from 1,000 to 2,000, this is a better result than the Facebook initiative, which increased total fans from 5,500 to 6,000. The Facebook community will likely still be contributing more leads, but the effect of the blogging initiative is greater because it added more net members to the community. This increase in community size will have an awareness payback over many months, or even years.

Figure 8.5 – **Community Growth**

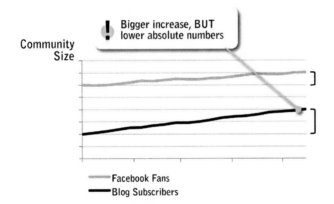

Awareness—Comparing Earned Efforts

With this flywheel dynamic in mind, we can compare our efforts to earn awareness against one another. As with paid efforts, there is an effectiveness and an efficiency element to this benchmarking, but the nature of earned awareness leads to some slight differences. Unlike paid awareness campaigns, earned awareness usually involves a community with an active set of discussions—the awareness it generates is much more indirect. To measure its overall effectiveness, let's compare traffic, inquiries, and MQLs against the audience (or community size).

Looking at the following chart, we can see that, in a given period, LinkedIn and Twitter are showing very different profiles. LinkedIn drives very little traffic, but a large number of MQLs, while Twitter drives significant traffic, but very few MQLs.

Figure 8.6 – **Comparing Effectiveness of Earned Efforts**

Campaign	Facebook Fans	Online Community Portal	LinkedIn Group	Twitter Audience
Audience	15000	33000	2000	8000
Traffic	1400	2500	100	1200
Traffic Effectiveness	9.3%	7.6%	5.0%	15.0%
Inquiries	140	240	50	80
Inquiry Effectiveness	10%	10%	50%	7%
MQLs	30	54	24	12
MQL Effectiveness	21%	23%	48%	15%
Community MQL Effectiveness	0.20%	0.16%	1.20%	0.15%

> **!** Twitter drives 12x more traffic BUT LinkedIn outperforms significantly on MQLs delivered

Benchmarking earned awareness efforts on a cost efficiency basis, however, is more challenging. First, the costs involved are generally people and permission costs, with (usually) few hard costs. Approximating these costs can be difficult, because active communities often have many people within the organization engaging on a regular basis.

Secondly, the "flywheel" nature of earned awareness makes it difficult to allocate costs. In any time period, efforts to build the community are split between engaging existing members and broadening the community. The cleanest way to allocate costs is to look at the percentage growth of the community on a quarterly basis. Split the costs in "maintenance" *vs.* "growth" in the same proportion as the community's growth percentage. The cost of the traffic, inquiries, and MQLs generated by the community should only be reflected in "maintenance" costs, since growth will show benefit in future quarters. This cost allocation means that a fast-growing community has most of its costs allocated against growth, making the current quarter results appear more economical.

The chart on page 202 extends the previous chart to add the cost of efforts in each medium, as well as the growth and maintenance breakout needed to correctly model the flywheel effect of growth. By doing this, we can see that Twitter becomes a much more cost-effective medium because of its high growth and low costs.

Interest to Inquiry: Comparing Marketing Assets

Each way you guide and facilitate discovery can bring prospective buyers to your website or Web properties. While this interest alone can drive prospects to engage with your sales team, in all likelihood buyers will need to be proactively nurtured with high-quality content over a period of time before they begin to actively seek solutions in your market space. Without this proactive

Figure 8.7 – Comparing Efficiency of Earned Efforts

Campaign	Facebook Fans	Online Community Portal	LinkedIn Group	Twitter Audience
Cost Per Quarter	$9,500	$18,000	$14,000	$5,500
Audience	15,000	33,000	2000	8000
Growth Percentage	9.3%	7.6%	14.0%	40.0%
Maintainence Cost	$8,613	$16,636	$12,040	$3,300
Growth Cost	$887	$1,364	$1,960	$2,200
Cost per Inquiry	$62	$69	$241	$41
Cost per MQL	$287	$308	$502	$275

> **!** Fast growth and low costs of Twitter make it a good MQL growth source

nurturing, you are dependent on other forms of passive discovery that can be more expensive and less targeted, such as advertising.

However, before you engage with and nurture prospects, they first must provide permission and contact information. Unfortunately, the simple act of requesting this information (e.g. before you provide a marketing asset) can lead to a significant fall-off in view rates (as opposed to "open access" where no request is made of the visitor). But in most instances, the value of adding that individual to the marketing database and the potential of longer term nurturing merits us making the simple request. Frankly, if the visitor is unwilling to share that basic information, she is inherently defining herself as an unqualified lead.

To optimize this conversion point, we must make an assessment: which assets can convince visitors to complete a form—and which don't present enough perceived value to persuade a visitor to complete the form? This will vary by industry and competitive landscape and will (and should) change over time. As more information becomes freely available, we must ensure that the value of what we withhold behind the Web form is high enough to avoid disappointing the visitor ("I completed all of that contact information—for *this?*").

To determine which assets can justify a gating form, test each asset type both with and without a "gatekeeper" form in front of it. Compare the number of visitors who view the landing page that describes the asset with the number who go on to view the asset itself. For non-gated assets, this conversion should be very high. What does the addition of a gating form do to the conversion rate? It will drop significantly, of course. However, those who do complete the form are, by definition, more interested and are worth adding to the marketing database. The conversion rate and the percentage of inquiries that are net new names give us a good sense of which assets/categories are sufficiently interesting to prospective buyers.

In the following chart, based on this analysis, we can see that whitepapers do not have enough perceived value to drive visitors to fill out a form because a precipitous

drop-off is seen. However, both webinars and client testimonials do merit the visitor's time. Webinars, although
seeing some drop-off, drive a large portion of net-new-
name growth, and are worth keeping gated.

Figure 8.8 – **Comparing Marketing Assets**

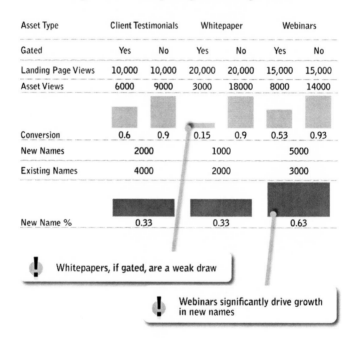

Asset Type	Client Testimonials		Whitepaper		Webinars	
Gated	Yes	No	Yes	No	Yes	No
Landing Page Views	10,000	10,000	20,000	20,000	15,000	15,000
Asset Views	6000	9000	3000	18000	8000	14000
Conversion	0.6	0.9	0.15	0.9	0.53	0.93
New Names	2000		1000		5000	
Existing Names	4000		2000		3000	
New Name %	0.33		0.33		0.63	

! Whitepapers, if gated, are a weak draw

! Webinars significantly drive growth in new names

Comparison of Outputs

Comparing alternative investments must also involve a
careful analysis of the intended outcomes. This might
seem obvious, but we often see confusion between what
is easily measured and what is relevant. For instance,
compare a tradeshow investment with an investment
in paid search. On the surface, it looks like both efforts
strive to drive new inquiries and create net new names
in the marketing database, but that may not be the case.

Tradeshow participation often involves a combination of early-stage Awareness, mid-stage Investigation, and late-stage Deal Acceleration. We won't have an accurate measurement if the only metric is inquiries or net new names (as it would likely be with paid search). Many tradeshow visitors are already known—they're already in the marketing database. Meeting with them at a show booth, however, is a valuable opportunity to investigate whether an opportunity has arisen since the last engagement.

Similarly, a tradeshow is often a great opportunity for scheduled or *ad hoc* meetings among key decision makers and executives. It might otherwise have taken much more effort to arrange and carry out those meetings, which are useful for moving deals to the next stage of the sales funnel.

Collectively, a tradeshow analysis must account for all intended outputs—short- and long-term. Benchmarking can only be done against the right set of investments. In the comparison below, we see that, measured against the most measurable metric (inquiries), a tradeshow investment appears less effective than a paid search campaign. However, when the outputs of the tradeshow investment are more fairly analyzed, we see that creating new inquiries is only one of three outputs. The conversations at the booth are comparable to a webinar in creating new SQOs. The executive conversations compare with field sales calls in their ability to move active opportunities from stage D to stage C.

Figure 8.9 – Comparing Marketing Outputs

	Option A	Total	Option B			Total
	Tradeshow		Search Spend	Webinars	Field Sales Meetings	
Financial Investment	50,000	35,000	20,000	5000		25,000
Time Investment	10,000	10,000		5000	15,000	20,000
Inquiries	1000	1000	1000			1000
SQOs	50	50		50		50
Sales Stage [d] ••▶ [c]	5	5			5	5

! Tradeshow may produce spectrum of outputs, BUT requires strategic focus

Using this assessment model to compare our investments provides clarity regarding how a comparison of investments should be made. At the same time, however, we can focus on the event that ensures the right strategic approach. For example, if the value of a tradeshow lies in its efficiency in arranging executive meetings, we must do appropriate pre-work to maximize these meetings.

Revenue Impact as a Common Metric for Comparing Campaigns

Often, as seen in the tradeshow example, the only way to fairly compare different investments is to make a comparison against a basket of tactical alternatives. To simplify this, there is often a temptation to compare campaigns against a common metric of revenue created.

This comparison challenge plagues many marketers because campaigns differ in their overall impact on buyers' progress toward a purchase decision. To compare disparate efforts using the common metric of revenue, there are a number of comparison models. Each has its own benefits and drawbacks. No model is more correct than any other. They merely offer different perspectives on the assessment of a campaign's value. The four most popular methods for benchmarking one campaign against another are:

- **Influenced Revenue**—The sum of all revenue that the campaign influenced.

- **Funnel Value Change**—The change in the value of the buying funnel because of the campaign.

- **Attributed Revenue**—The effect of a campaign based on the unique association of each deal with a single campaign, or shared proportionately across multiple campaigns.

- **Campaign Focus Map**—A visualization of the main buying stage area of effect of each campaign in order to select the right campaign for a given initiative

Many organizations find that a single comparison methodology is right for their business. This depends on the complexity and length of the buying process, the number of individuals on the buying team, and the goals of the comparison.

Comparing Influenced Revenue

The Influenced Revenue methodology looks at the total revenue that each campaign affected. The first step is to identify the individual buyers each campaign affected. This is done using an "influence threshold" for each marketing type. For example, an e-mail may influence an individual if he clicks on a link in the e-mail—but not if he merely opens the e-mail. A webinar influences an attendee if she stays for more than five minutes—but not if she merely registers.

Using this influence threshold, we can see how each campaign influenced a list of individual buyers. If those buyers are involved in a buying process that results in revenue, we say the campaign influenced that revenue. Tally up all revenue influenced by each campaign to get a perspective on which campaigns influenced more revenue.

Of course, this approach double-counts the revenue of a purchase that is influenced by multiple campaigns and makes no attempt to allocate revenue across the campaigns that influenced it. However, this simplicity can be a benefit because influenced revenue is simple to calculate. If all marketing campaigns under comparison focus at a similar stage of the funnel (such as the creation of net new awareness), we have a very efficient way to determine which campaigns merit further investment. This is also a useful methodology when marketing does not yet communicate with buyers throughout the entire buying process.

If, however, campaigns under comparison target different stages of the buying process, and marketing has a broad communication footprint that interacts with buyers throughout the buying process, the influenced revenue methodology may simplify the comparison too much to be of use.

Comparing Funnel Value Change

To compare marketing campaigns that affect different areas of the buying funnel, other methodologies are

Figure 8.10 – **Comparing Funnel Value Change**

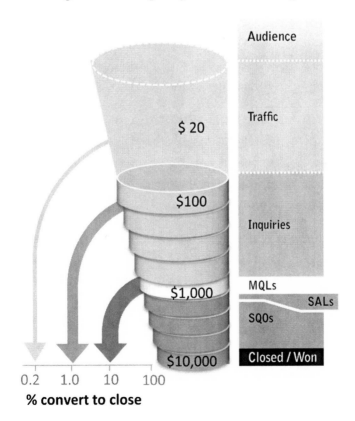

useful. With the buying funnel stages modeled, and an appropriate model for defining what marketing action causes which changes in the funnel (see Chapter 6), we can compare marketing campaigns based on changes in funnel value. To do so, assess the value of a lead at each stage based on the value of a closed transaction and reduce that value based on the conversion rates from each stage through to close.

Based on this assessment of a lead's true value at each stage of the buying process, we can assess the change in funnel value caused by each campaign. Some campaigns generate sales-ready leads while others drive business to close. Still others add new interest to the top of the funnel. Regardless of goal, each campaign's value can be assessed using the same overall framework.

Similarly, we can calculate the true cost of each campaign by including hard costs, people costs, and permission costs (the cost of pushing uninterested recipients one step closer to dis-engagement). This gives us a standard basis to compare costs across campaigns.

For example, if a campaign costs $50,000 and moves 1,000 leads from "inactive name" (worth $20) to "mildly interested" (worth $100), pushes 10 leads from "mildly interested" to MQL status (worth $1,000), and creates 200 new "mildly interested" leads not previously in the marketing database, the value of the marketing campaign can be calculated as:

Value of Campaign:

1,000 X ($100—$20) = $80,000

10 X ($1,000—$10) = $9,000

200 X $100 = $20,000

==================

Total: $109,000

Clearly, if we only look at the creation of qualified leads, the value of the campaign appears to be very low—but in reality, it was a very successful and valuable campaign that triggered a lot of valuable early funnel re-engagement of inactive names and generated new interest.

This analysis allows us to look at marketing campaigns in a new light, as in the following chart. We see that the end-of-year sale generated $10,000 in revenue for only $5,000 in hard costs, but it also drove a large number of people toward disengagement, leading to a significant permission cost. With this factored in, it becomes one of the worst-performing campaigns.

Figure 8.11 – Comparing Return on Investment

Campaign	Webinar Series	Industry Tradeshow	Industry Blog	End of Year Sale
Hard Cost	30,000	20,000	5000	5000
Permission Cost	7000	10000	0	30,000
People Cost	3000	5000	15,000	5000
Total Cost	40,000	35,000	20,000	40,000
Funnel Increase	50,000	70,000	30,000	10,000
ROI	25%	100%	50%	-75%

Comparing Attributed Revenue

The concept of attributed revenue attempts to avoid the double-counting of the influenced revenue method by "attributing" the revenue from a deal to one or more marketing campaigns, using a defined pattern. Three of the most common attribution patterns are:

- **First Touch:** The revenue is attributed to the campaign that first touched one of the prospect's stakeholders in the deal. This attribution pattern is best when awareness is your largest challenge and your marketing campaigns mainly focus on generating net new interest and connecting with early-stage prospects.

- **Last Touch (before Opportunity):** Here, we attribute the revenue to the campaign that last touched an individual in the buying group prior to the opportunity being identified. This pattern is best when your primary challenge is finding and driving active buying processes in a large marketing database. This pattern identifies the most likely message to trigger or identify buying behavior.

- **Even:** In this model, we attribute the revenue across all campaigns that influence buyers within the buying center. This pattern is ideal when you must nurture and educate buyers for long periods before the buying process starts. This pattern identifies key messages in the nurture content that effected buyer motivation.

Attributed revenue methods analyze the impact of individual marketing campaigns on the sales cycle and final revenue, which is why it is best when there is no extreme variability in the length and effectiveness of the sales cycle. Variability can obscure the analysis of the effect of marketing campaigns. In such cases, funnel-value change may be the preferred methodology.

Figure 8.12 – Comparing Attributed Revenue

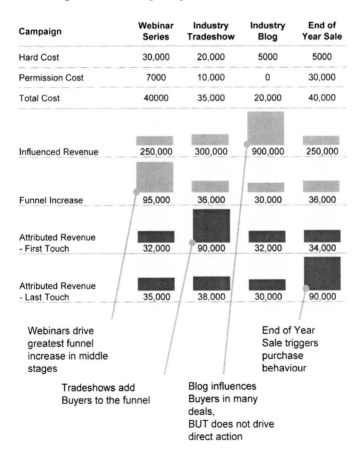

Campaign	Webinar Series	Industry Tradeshow	Industry Blog	End of Year Sale
Hard Cost	30,000	20,000	5000	5000
Permission Cost	7000	10,000	0	30,000
Total Cost	40000	35,000	20,000	40,000
Influenced Revenue	250,000	300,000	900,000	250,000
Funnel Increase	95,000	36,000	30,000	36,000
Attributed Revenue - First Touch	32,000	90,000	32,000	34,000
Attributed Revenue - Last Touch	35,000	38,000	30,000	90,000

Webinars drive greatest funnel increase in middle stages

Tradeshows add Buyers to the funnel

Blog influences Buyers in many deals, BUT does not drive direct action

End of Year Sale triggers purchase behaviour

Each methodology highlights a different area of effect. Each business, depending on its revenue engine challenges, will adopt a methodology, or methodologies, that makes the most sense for best comparing campaigns in light of those unique challenges.

Comparing Campaign Focus

Each of the preceding methodologies analyzes a marketing campaign based on the value it contributes to the organization. As important as this is, it is also quite valuable to understand campaign focus for substantially different campaigns by visualizing where in the funnel they caused change.

Since each campaign changes the funnel (often at multiple points), visualizing this effect allows us to choose the campaign that optimally targets a particular challenge in the funnel. To do this, we must look at each campaign from the perspective of what change it causes. Again, this can be defined using a minimum threshold of influence and looking at any campaign that influences the buying process in the week prior to a change.

The main points of the buying process—traffic, inquiries, MQLs, and closed/won opportunities—can be mapped against the stage of the buying funnel where they have an effect. With a metric of the total change in funnel value, we see where each campaign is truly having an effect. For example, if we mainly want to focus on growing awareness, the thought leader video campaign is the one to emulate. If inquiries and MQLs are in

demand, the webinar campaign is the best option. And
the ROI analysis tool is most effective in guiding deals to
close. Each campaign type serves a unique purpose, and
this view of the effect of each campaign provides the best
way to select the optimum style for your specific revenue
engine challenge.

Figure 8.13 – **Comparing Campaign Focus**

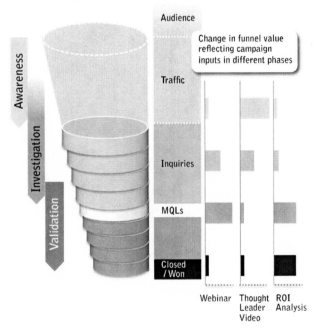

Comparing Deal Sources

Let's use a similar exercise to view the revenue engine
from the opposite direction. We'll look at the number of
deals, revenue, and average deal size of closed deals and
connect it back to where the deal was originally sourced
to identify the most successful initial touches. Like we

did in the campaign comparison, we'll use an attribution methodology to categorize deals. Often, this view uses first-touch attribution, but is can use last-touch equally effectively.

Looking at final deals and deal sizes, we can identify the major categories of sources. Marketing, sales, and partners will be our deal sources. Or we can benchmark against major go-to-market strategies based on their ability to source deals and revenues.

Figure 8.14 – **Comparing Lead Source by First Touch**

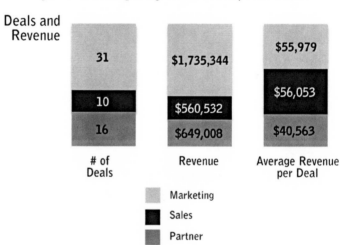

It's challenging to compare campaigns and judge their abilities to move buyers through a lengthy process, but an integrated revenue performance management strategy offers numerous ways to benchmark performance. Any business needs multiple methods of benchmarking to obtain new insights into campaign performance and make critical allocation decisions. There is no one correct method of comparison. Each method offers its unique view on one aspect of comparative performance.

Comparing Content and Message Alternatives

Although the overall view of lead flows through the funnel is essential we mustn't overlook the importance of our ability to measure the effectiveness of our messages that guide buyer perceptions. Marketing generally works hard to provide both online content/messaging as well as content/ messaging for use by sales teams as they engage buyers.

> **Case Example**
>
> With a fully revamped website that was an invaluable resource throughout the buying process, the FifthThird bank marketing team began promoting it to an unlikely audience; their own sales team. An internal marketing campaign was designed that introduced different areas and resources on the website to the sales team, showing them both how it could be used in an engagement with a buyer, and what it might mean if a buyer was seen to engage with that resource.
>
> By adding this educational effort to their marketing, the FifthThird bank team deepened their engagement with sales and began to optimize what content assets were being created through understanding what assets were being used, and how. Similarly, the sales team began to leverage the online assets in their sales engagements, and in doing so, generated much deeper insights into buyer behavior than would have otherwise been generated.

This direct use by the sales team represents a valuable test bed for understanding which messages are most effective in guiding buyers. For example, the following chart shows that the Product Spec Sheet has not been discovered by the sales team, while the ROI calculator is frequently viewed by sales, but is not being used. The Video Testimonials are being used frequently, but aren't connecting with the buying audience, while the Technical Specifications, although used less frequently, are well-received by recipients.

Figure 8.15 – **Comparing Asset Usage and Effectiveness**

Content	Sales Views	Total Sends	Open %	Click %
Financial Services Case Study	46	44	43%	14%
Product Spec Sheet	8	7	45%	14%
ROI Calculator	80	8	40%	12%
Technical Specifications	42	38	85%	40%
Video Testimonials	80	72	20%	0.5%

This ability to assess content usage is key to understanding the perceived need of messages within your sales team's audience. Since they directly connect with prospective buyers, this usage history is a clear indicator of their view of the overall market's messaging needs. Combined with the insights this provides into market reception of messages, this dashboard view lets you direct marketing efforts at only the most highly leveraged content investments.

Benchmarking Sales Rep Performance

Once the sales team receives an MQL, the success of the resulting cycle then becomes dependent on the individual salesperson whose performance is determined and measured by a number of factors. The performance of each sales professional should be benchmarked against a team average (or perhaps the average performance of a select group of high performers). If significant variances exist, further investigation can identify whether there is a performance challenge with that individual.

Like our analysis of the pipeline, the analysis of an individual sales rep's performance should include the pipeline size, shape, and average age (as an indicator of speed) to pinpoint where to localize issues. A low conversion rate or significant blockage can indicate issues either in rep skills, rep performance, or lead flow to that territory.

> **Case Example**
>
> Equally problematic as territories with too few leads were territories with too many leads. Analysis of the MQL to SQO process had shown Platts that leads not followed up on in within 48hrs had nearly zero chance of converting. Based on this, when territories were being provided with too many leads and were beginning to miss their agreed call-back times, the Platts team reduced the marketing investments in those territories and reallocated that investment elsewhere. Rather than see unproductive sales people and frustrated buyers, Platts focused marketing effort on territories where the lead flow was lower.

In the following comparison chart, for example, we can see that Sally Smith is performing noticeably worse than the team average at converting deals to the Solution Proposal stage, which may be indicative of a skills issue.

Figure 8.16 – **Benchmarking Sales Rep Performance**

		Sally Smith			Team average			Variance		
		Size	Age	CR	Size	Age	CR	Size	Age	CR
MQLs		100			80			0.25		20
SALs		70		70%	48		60%	0.46		10%
SQOs	e Needs Analysis	50	30	71%	28	30	58%	0.79	0	13%
	d Solution Presentation	40	60	80%	14	40	50%	1.86	0.5	30%
	c Solution Proposal	8	40	20%	6	50	43%	0.33	-0.2	-23%
	b Commitment /Negotiation	4	60	50%	3	60	50%	0.33	0	0%
	a Closed Won	2	70	50%	2	70	67%	0	0	-17%

CR = Conversion Rate

! More moving to Stage D, BUT challenges moving to Stage C

In addition, at each stage in the sales process, the data obtained by looking at buyers' digital body language can provide insights far deeper than sales-reported insights alone:

- MQL to SAL: Variance here suggests challenges following the hand-off process between marketing and sales. It can also indicate that this salesperson's territory is receiving lower-quality MQLs.

- SAL to SQO (Stage E): Underperformance here may indicate that the salesperson is unable to initiate conversations that precisely target the pain points of the buyer. It may also indicate a lack of

Case Example

While search was a key component of Platts' process for being discovered by buyers, analysis indicated that it was most often leveraged early in the buyer's process. Those who discovered Platts in this manner were often six months to a year away from a purchase decision. For this reason, the Platts team decided to route the majority of inquiries from search into a nurturing program, rather than directly to sales. Over time, the buyers interest and education level increased, and when buying signals were detected, a salesperson was brought into the conversation. Keep in mind Platts always offered a faster but secondary path to conversion for those few individuals who were farther along in the buying process.

focus on translating the buyer's digital body language into pain points and conversation starters.

- Stage E (Needs Analysis) to Stage D (Solution Presentation): The sales rep may be failing to convey viable solutions for key pain points. Examine both buyer activity and content usage patterns to determine if the discussion of solutions differs from your top-performing reps.

- Stage D (Solution Presentation) to Stage C (Solution Proposal): An inability to reach the Solution Proposal phase often indicates an inability to access the right decision makers. You'll likely see differences in the engagement of key decision makers compared to similar stage accounts managed by your top sales professionals.

- Stage C (Solution Proposal) to Stage B (Commitment and Negotiation): A variance here often shows an inability to gain the overall commitment of a buying team. Look for differences in overall team engagement, and engagement with typical blockers to identify whether key objections are being overcome correctly.

- Stage B (Commitment and Negotiation) to Stage A (Closed/Won): Examine any variance to spot any negotiating-skills deficiency. Examine buyer behavior to identify indications of early-stage interest that indicate the deal was prematurely marked as committed to the proposal.

While each territory and salesperson is different, analyzing your team and pipeline in this way—and with an eye to the digital body language of buyers in the deal—allows you to properly benchmark your sales team against top performers and the team average.

Benchmarking Against a Plan

We can only continue to improve sales performance if there is an end-to-end plan that clearly conveys what the size, shape, and speed of the revenue engine should be. This level of benchmark *planning*, more so than the actual benchmarking of alternatives against one another, lets us see unintended effects and consequences. Often what we expect will be strong improvement in one area of the revenue engine (such as driving a large number of new inquiries) has an unintended downstream effect (such as overloading the sales team and decreasing their effectiveness) that minimizes or even negates its impact on new revenue. Benchmarking against a comprehensive plan exposes these potential shortcomings.

Top-Down Planning

Carefully planning all aspects of the end-to-end revenue engine and creating a single view of that engine means addressing a number of complexities that have been explored in some depth. However, as an executive level dashboard, this top-down plan offers tremendous value by providing the structure and skeleton for the more detailed plans that address each subordinate section. Your overall plan—showing the progress of buyers from the earliest stages to deal closure—should include a number of important elements:

Time

To account for time/speed, loosely approximate when a time transition must occur. Given the nature of business, we can count on a certain level of traffic, inquiries, MQLs, and deals throughout a quarter. But a plan represents a quarter as a defined number. By selecting a stage of the revenue engine to make a defined transition from one quarter to the next, this effect of time can be represented fairly effectively.

For example, if the marketing team must generate 1,000 MQLs in a quarter, and its campaigns are spread throughout a quarter, it may be reasonable to shift between quarters when, in the plan, MQLs transition to SALs. Similarly, if sales often takes 90 days from lead to close, it makes sense to add another quarterly shift between SQO and Closed/Won.

In this diagram, we can see the time-lag effect of deals progressing from the earliest stages to the latest stages with a quarter of elapsed time between major stages.

Figure 8.17 – **Top-Down Planning**

Stage	Q1	Q2	Q3	Q4
Audience	3,000,000	3,600,000	4,200,000	4,800,000
Traffic		1,050,000	1,200,000	1,350,000
Inquiries		27,000	32,000	38,000
Prospects (Active)		250,000	300,000	350,000
MQLs		9,000	10,000	11,000
SALs			6,500	7,300
SQOs	e		3,900	4,600
Closed Won	a			610

Natural Traffic

While we can track the effectiveness of many efforts to drive traffic to Web properties, most of it may still appear either naturally or from unknown sources. In an end-to-end plan, this can either be represented separately, or combined with more explicitly sourced traffic, but it is an important effect to be cognizant of.

Inquiries and the Database

Similarly, the transition from newly sourced inquiries and MQLs must take into account the effect of nurturing the existing marketing database.

Designing for Awareness

In building a marketing plan for the Awareness stage, the most effective approach is often to split awareness into passive, active, and influence-based discovery. For each way of influencing awareness, create a plan to measure the audience size, interest driven, and inquiries captured. While many factors contribute to the success of these programs under this level of planning, these metrics give a clear indication of what is possible, and whether there is an improvement quarter over quarter.

Active Discovery

Active discovery of information is often the easiest to model. The audience size is the number of relevant search queries—which is the maximum number of people seeking information on topics relevant to your solution. There are two ways to affect this number over time. First, the list of relevant search terms can be updated. If, for example, a medical devices company broadens where it would ideally be found from "X-ray imaging" to "medical imaging," it will increase the number of searches seen as relevant. However, unless there is significant work to convert those inquiries, subsequent conversion rates will likely decrease.

Success in paid (SEM) and organic (SEO) search efforts will bring interested traffic to your Web properties. This traffic will increase even more if you offer more search-discoverable assets that enable more long-tail searches to find your content. Alternatively, you can increase your SEM budget.

After you drive interest to your Web properties, the next step is to convert those visitors into inbound inquiries by offering a content asset of sufficient value that persuades the individual to interact. This conversion ratio has perhaps the most flexibility in the planning process. If your main challenge is to increase overall awareness, you want to keep this ratio low and offer much of your content available without requiring a registration form. This ungated content is also much more likely to be shared among peers and colleagues. However, if awareness is not your challenge, and your organic Web traffic is already very high, you can "gate" the access to a subset of higher-value content assets in order to persuade visitors to self-convert into inquiries.

Passive Discovery

Passive discovery is a bit trickier because it is slightly less trackable. However, with modeling and planning we can move our passive-discovery awareness efforts from art to science. Again, as with active discovery. The three key factors to model are: audience size, interest driven, and inquiries generated. For example, if your passive-discovery awareness efforts mainly focus around advertising, you can model these three factors using the number of ad impressions generated, the amount of traffic driven to your Web properties or landing pages, and the number of inquiries generated from these efforts.

The number of ad impressions is, of course, a direct result of budget and targeting. Planning for growth, however, requires us to assess whether increasing our ad impressions would significantly reduce conversion rates (because relevance would erode). With an advertising plan in place, conversion rates will be similar to the rates from active discovery, such as search. If the ad directs visitors to a conversion-oriented experience (e.g. a landing page with an asset that is gated by a request form), you may see higher conversion rates, but less organic sharing of the content. However, if the ad drives viewers to ungated content, the conversion numbers may decrease, but the overall traffic may be higher.

Influence-Based Discovery

Although it can often be the most critical factor in marketing success, influence-based discovery is also the most difficult to measure. However, the same high-level framework holds true for potential audience, traffic, and inquiries. Each key influencer holds an influence over an audience of a specific size. While this cannot be measured with 100-percent accuracy, for our planning purposes, if we use a consistent measure—such as social network size, blog traffic, or distribution—we can measure and analyze it with confidence. An influencer strategy should start with a good approximation of each influencer's audience reach. This estimate will help us

> **Case Example**
>
> Measuring the development of influence through personal brands is challenging, so Informatica mainly measures the more tangible metrics. The number of followers each market advocate has in each relevant medium, the number of interactions (comments, questions, or Tweets), and the amount of content created all give indicators of the amount, if not the quality, of each advocate's engagement with the market. By ensuring that this interaction was focused across the known influencers in the market, the Informatica team noticed many examples of influencers whose perspectives had been altered. In one particularly telling example, Informatica advocates used online interactions to build a relationship with a consultant who was recognized as an expert in a competitive product. This relationship quickly led to a face to face meeting, which allowed a new perspective on Informatica to be shared. Almost immediately, the consultant published a very positive article on Informatica's products to his audience.

decide whether to focus on better relations with a core group of influencers, or build more relationships with a broader set of influencers.

Traffic and inquiries from influencers should be measured as an indicator of successful engagement with the influencer channel than as a direct source of leads. While a successful engagement strategy and smart content creation will lead to referred traffic from influencers, their desire to be perceived as neutral restricts this flow significantly. However, as an executive-level proxy for their sentiment, and likelihood to include you in the conversation, it is a good measure.

In the following chart, many of these trends can be seen. Broadening out the search queries to new terms results in more traffic and inquiries, but qualification through to MQL should be watched carefully. At the same time, traffic from ads remains flat but is driving more

Figure 8.18 – **Planning for Discovery**

Awareness	Q1		Q2		Q3	
	Number	CR%	Number	CR%	Number	CR%
Active Audience (Search Queries)	15,000		25,000		40,000	
Active Traffic (Search-Driven)	1500	10%	2500	10%	4000	10%
Active Inquiries (Search-Driven)	300	20%	500	20%	800	20%
Passive Audience (Ad Impressions)	10,000		10,000		10,000	
Passive Traffic (Ad Driven)	1000	10%	1000	10%	1000	10%
Passive Inquiries (Ad Driven)	100	10%	150	15%	250	25%
Influencer Audience (Community Size)	20,000		30,000		40,000	
Influencer Traffic	200	1%	600	2%	1600	4%
Influencer Inquiries	40	20%	120	20%	320	20%
Total Inquiries	440		770		1370	

CR = Conversion Rate

Rapid growth in search queries likely means less relevance; conversion rates may suffer.

Growing conversion rates this fast may have adverse effect on how your content is shared with influencers.

Trying to push influencers to be a direct source of leads may backfire. Treat traffic as an indicator of success.

inquiries as the gating with Web forms is tightened. This may result in less secondary sharing of the assets.

Modeling Conversion

After building a plan to measure and drive awareness efforts, our next step is to create a high-level plan to guide that traffic into becoming a qualified lead. However, since the buying process is governed by the prospect's level of interest, this must be done by carefully nurturing early-stage interest, watching for signs of deeper investigation, and being careful not to drive audiences away through over-communication.

The input for this plan is the net new inquiries that drive the growth of the marketing database. This initial indicator of interest provides a starting point for nurturing prospects to discover the timing of their buying process and areas of interest that define a qualified lead. While the techniques and messaging to nurture prospects vary widely, at a high level, what counts are fit and engagement. The two dimensions of fit and engagement, as discussed earlier, form the key dimensions on which we analyze the overall marketing database.

Fit—the demographic and firmographic criteria of a buyer that makes her qualified to purchase—is an important planning dimension. If a marketing database grows, but does so with the wrong types of names, subsequent messaging will not be of interest to recipients. If marketing database growth pursues only raw numbers, but is not driving growth in the ideal market segments, we will need to revisit our awareness efforts in order to increase our appeal to the intended audience.

Engagement—the second crucial dimension—refers to the signs of buying interest shown by the prospect. Positive engagement trends in your marketing database can indicate either a surge in market interest in your solutions, or highly relevant content that is connecting with buyers. Negative trends in engagement show the opposite—usually when there's been over-communication, or the content is overly sales-oriented communication, which drives away buying audiences.

The output of this stage is, of course, qualified leads for sales. MQLs are based on a carefully defined agreement between marketing and sales regarding the appropriate fit and engagement levels. If, for example, there is an agreement that A1, A2, B1, and C1 levels qualify, then each name in that category is an MQL. Worth watching closely, however, are the numbers that make up the MQL total. If too many leads of the lowest acceptable level of qualification (C1) pass through, it will cause problems in the sales organization.

Lead Nurturing and Conversion Plans

One of the central tenets of modern revenue performance management is the concept that buyers control their own buying processes. This means that the revenue organization should work to facilitate and detect active buying processes—but it can do very little to conjure up a buying process where one does not already exist.

Figure 8.19 – Modeling Conversion

Callouts:
- Great database growth, ahead of plan
- But growth is in names with poor fit to target buyer

Investigation		Q1	Q2		Q3		Q4	
		Actual	Actual	Growth %	Actual	Growth %	Actual	Growth %
Total Names		100000	120000	20%	140000	17%	160000	14%
Names by Fit	D	25000	40000	60%	50000	25%	60000	20%
	C	25000	30000	20%	40000	33%	50000	25%
	B	25000	25000	0%	25000	0%	25000	0%
	A	25000	25000	0%	25000	0%	25000	0%
Names by Engagement	4	70000	89000	27%	106000	19%	122000	15%
	3	15000	18000	20%	23000	28%	28500	24%
	2	10000	9000	-10%	8000	-11%	7000	-13%
	1	5000	4000	-20%	3000	-25%	2500	-17%
Qualified Leads	C1	100	150	50%	210	40%	270	29%
	B1	100	150	50%	210	40%	270	29%
	A2	100	100	0%	90	-10%	80	-11%
	A1	100	100	0%	90	-10%	80	-11%
Total Qualified Leads	MQLs	400	500	25%	600	20%	700	17%

Callouts:
- Lack of fit, or over-communication may be leading to disengagement; highly engaged numbers decreasing
- Although total MQL numbers are on track, quality is decreasing significantly, likely leading to sales challenges

If this is the case, it's difficult to see how this can fuel accurate planning assumptions. However, a top-down view helps us form accurate approximations. With a good lead-nurturing program in place, a percentage of prospective buyers will, based on events in their own business, become active in any given quarter. This approximate range of engagement can be a very valuable planning assumption. If this level of engagement holds across all levels of fit (another testable assumption), the number of A1 leads is determined from a combination of the database of A names, combined with the percentage of well-nurtured leads that typically show Level 1 engagement in any given quarter.

A similar analysis for every other MQL qualification level shows approximately how many MQLs we can expect to be developed as a result of nurturing the prospect database. To grow this number we must either optimize the nurturing programs or expand the database of A and B names through more early-stage (and earlier-stage) awareness efforts.

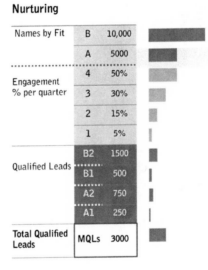

Figure 8.20 **Lead Nurturing and Conversion Plans**

Nurturing

Names by Fit	B	10,000	
	A	5000	
Engagement % per quarter	4	50%	
	3	30%	
	2	15%	
	1	5%	
Qualified Leads	B2	1500	
	B1	500	
	A2	750	
	A1	250	
Total Qualified Leads	MQLs	3000	

Projecting Handoffs

Once an active buying process has been uncovered, and an MQL is confirmed, we must ensure the sales team is invited to the table to help facilitate the consideration. Without this crucial step, the buyer's process for

Case Example

As the FifthThird bank team began their journey towards a new way of engaging with buyers, it was important to ensure that all their Investment Advisors were bought in to the new strategy. At the time, Investment Advisors had no efficient way to communicate with their private clients except for time consuming one on one conversations. Realizing this, the marketing team began capturing a weekly video of their senior economic advisor sharing his observations on the market. This video was shared with FifthThird private clients through a weekly newsletter distribution.

Shortly after this process started, the Investment Advisors who had entered their private clients into the program began reporting a significant increase in inbound calls from their clients. While the content of the communication was purely educational it had the effect of keeping FifthThird bank, and their Investment Advisor, top of mind. This quickly translated to inbound calls as private clients took the initiative to call their advisor and discuss a transaction they had been considering.

validating solution choices will likely be guided by competitors who are more engaged with key stakeholders.

Handing off a MQL to the sales team means that lead must be accepted by sales as valid and qualified. After an initial conversation, sales must determine that a qualified opportunity exists. The first measurement of this process, the SAL/MQL ratio, indicates the alignment between the marketing and sales teams around the criteria being used to qualify leads. If the SAL/MQL ratio is too low, it indicates that sales does not agree with the MQL definitions, or is not actively following up the leads they get from marketing.

The ratio of SQOs to SALs, however, reveals whether buyers are truly ready to engage with a salesperson to drive a sales transaction. If this ratio is too low, many of the leads being handed off to sales are not truly ready. That is, they are individuals who have been scored, qualified, and accepted by sales, but are not turning into opportunities. If this is the case, you will likely benefit from revisiting the definition of a qualified lead.

In the following chart, we can see aggressive growth in both MQL numbers and the conversion rate to SQO. This results in a near doubling of SQOs in two quarters. Unless the sales team is staffed for this increase, this may result in stuck deals early in the pipeline as there is no sales bandwidth to manage each deal.

Figure 8.21 – **Projecting Hand-offs**

Closing	Q1		Q2			Q3		
Lead Handoff	Actual	CR%	Plan	Actual	Growth % (Actual)	Plan	Actual	Growth % (Plan)
MQLs	5000	-	6000	6000	-	7000	7000	-
SALs	3000	60%	3800	4200	70%	4500	5400	77%
SQOs	1000	33%	1200	1400	33%	1400	1800	33%

CR = Conversion Rate

 MQLs are growing, but lead acceptance (to SAL) is growing even faster – may cause deals to slow early in pipeline

Sales Prospecting and Latent Demand

Pipeline that's generated by marketing's efforts to nurture and grow the database creates the vast majority of the volume in an efficient and optimized revenue machine. However, in many market spaces, we still see tremendous value in having the sales team proactively contact inactive or low-potential prospects. This may seem counterintuitive, or even counterproductive. However, in certain cases, it can form a very valuable function. To see why, look all the way back to the methods of discovery that lead buyers to become aware of your solutions.

Active discovery, often via search, is the most enticing because it's a buyer actively seeking information about your solutions. Influenced discovery, often via social media, engages networks of peers to influence prospects outside of your immediate circle who have an interest in your space. Passive discovery, often via advertisements, catches prospects who are loosely interested in your space, but not actively seeking information.

But this leaves out one group of potential buyers: those who think they understand—and believe that they do not require—your products or services. Unless this viewpoint shifts, they will not actively seek to learn more—so they won't find themselves discussing relevant topics with influencers or intrigued by advertisements. These prospects are best engaged directly as a conversation that can provoke a fundamental shift in mindset that triggers or renews their interest in your space.

For this set of buyers, having your field or inside sales team directly call and cultivate interest may be the only way to start a buying conversation. To plan this type of lead flow, prospecting activity becomes a proxy for expected results. The ratio of the number of prospecting calls and one-to-one e-mails sent by each sales rep to the number of new opportunities generated provides a reasonable predictor of expected success. With this success ratio in mind, we can predict the number of sales-generated new opportunities based on managing to a specific level of prospecting activity.

Planning to Win

The final stage of the process is when sales helps the buying team reach a consensus, objections are overcome, and contract details are finalized. Planning for this stage involves analyzing the opportunity from sales' perspective managing the deal. Doing so, we can gain significant insights into many observable aspects of buyer behavior. It's critical to benchmark for this stage of the revenue process with a clear model of both where each deal is in the pipeline, and more importantly, how long it has been there. If opportunities are floundering in the early stages of discussion, either the leads were not ready for the sales team, or the sales team is unable to move them forward.

If we encounter this situation, we should look at the engagement level of the leads being sent to sales to ensure they are of sufficiently high quality. If the level of fit is good, but the level of engagement is low, there may not be a compelling business challenge to explore, so the deal remains stuck early in the pipeline for a long time.

If this is not the case, we should analyze whether pipeline performance differs significantly among sales team members to see if a sales skills issue is present.

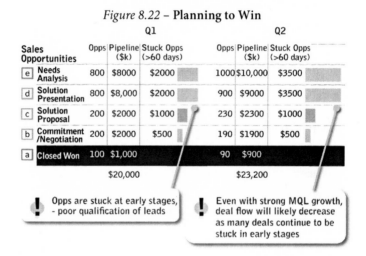

Figure 8.22 – **Planning to Win**

Sales Opportunities	Q1			Q2		
	Opps	Pipeline ($k)	Stuck Opps (>60 days)	Opps	Pipeline ($k)	Stuck Opps (>60 days)
e Needs Analysis	800	$8000	$2000	1000	$10,000	$3500
d Solution Presentation	800	$8,000	$2000	900	$9000	$3500
c Solution Proposal	200	$2000	$1000	230	$2300	$1000
b Commitment /Negotiation	200	$2000	$500	190	$1900	$500
a Closed Won	100	$1,000		90	$900	
		$20,000			$23,200	

> ❗ Opps are stuck at early stages, - poor qualification of leads

> ❗ Even with strong MQL growth, deal flow will likely decrease as many deals continue to be stuck in early stages

Pipeline Rollover

Next, we should turn our attention to the issue of pipeline rollover. As leads pass from marketing to sales, some will result in closed revenue, some will be lost or disqualified, and some will remain in the pipeline as active deals that roll into the next fiscal quarter. We must factor in these roll-over opportunities at the beginning of a quarter to understand the needs for the next quarter's SQOs.

To do this, we must look at each territory or rep, and understand their pipelines and what is likely to happen as the quarter transitions. Early-stage deals will not be part of the current quarter's pipeline and can be counted for what they are. However, late-stage deals may or may not close in the current quarter. If they do not, they may roll over into the following quarter.

Let's look at this from a single salesperson's perspective. If we have a $200,000 revenue plan for a quarter, we need a $1.2 million pipeline (assuming a 15 percent close rate from SQO, which leads to a 6x coverage multiplier). If $300,000 of the pipeline is early-stage, $900,000 of pipeline is still needed. If $200,000 of late-stage pipeline can be expected not to close in Q1, instead rolling over to Q2 as active opportunities, marketing needs to build $700,000 in SQOs for this salesperson. At an average selling price of $100,000, this means 7 SQOs.

Figure 8.23 – **Pipeline Rollover**

Q2 Revenue Plan	200,000
Coverage Multiplier	6X
Pipeline Needed	1,200,000
Pipeline "Have" (Early Stage)	300,000
Pipeline Gap (Need – Have)	900,000
Pipeline Rollover (Late Stage)	200,000
Pipeline Build (Gap – Rollover)	700,000
SQO's needed (Build/ASP ($100k))	7

Analyzing upcoming quarters this way allows us to better align their efforts on a rep-by-rep or territory-by-territory basis to ensure the sales pipeline in each region is optimized.

Planning Future Quarters

One of the most valuable outcomes in building a high-performance revenue engine is the ability to extend this planning exercise beyond typical detailed revenue planning timelines of the current and next fiscal quarter. The core of our new ability to provide detailed, bottom-up forecasts is the ability to forecast the inflow of SQOs into the sales pipeline. With conversion rates from SQO to Close remaining constant (for the sake of planning), future revenues are mainly a function of average deal age and the inflow of new SQOs. SQOs in any given quarter come mainly from three sources:

- New SQOs from MQLs created by the marketing team.

- Rollovers from previous quarters.

- Direct efforts from the sales team to generate their own opportunities by stimulating latent demand or provoking mindset shifts.

Each value can be individually planned for using the planning structures described above. In the aggregate, these form a predictable, long-range revenue forecast that has not been previously possible.

Figure 8.24 – **Planning Future Quarters**

SQO Sources	Q1	Q2	Q3	Q4
MQL driven	1000	1200	1400	1600
Pipeline Rollover	400	450	500	600
Sales Prospecting	200	225	250	275
Total SQOs	1600	1875	2150	2475
Conversion Rate	15%	15%	15%	15%
Average Deal Size	$100,000	$100,000	$100,000	$100,000
Revenue ($000s)	$24,000	$28,125	$32,250	$37,125

Comparing to the Best

With benchmarks in place to compare alternatives and evaluate performance against a plan, we can begin to understand and optimize the revenue engine holistically. In many cases, the additional visibility this provides can uncover hidden issues and opportunities to improve. However, as we deal with the obvious improvements, the question remains: where should we focus our ongoing optimization efforts?

The best way to make that determination is by comparing to what others have achieved in similar situations. Comparisons to best-in-class benchmarks, however, are limited by how well you define those comparable benchmarks. All industries, audiences, and solutions are unique, and comparisons among incompatible situations can lead to mistaken conclusions.

Tactical Comparisons

Often, our most practical comparisons are at the tactical level. Regardless of industry or audience, looking at the performance of specific tools can be beneficial. Tactical metrics such as open and clickthrough rates on different e-mailed webinar invitations can be feasibly compared with each other. Conversion rates from Web visitor traffic to Web form submissions can indicate what can be achieved and what the performance ranges might be. Metrics on the shape and conversion rates of the sales funnel can guide us to areas warranting further investigation.

While these tactical comparisons provide no adjustments for audiences, messages, or offers, they do offer a good sense of performance ranges to expect. Variances aren't necessarily good or bad, but we should understand whether the anomalies are expected based on audience, offer, or other factors, or if we have detected an opportunity to improve.

Horizontal Comparisons

A more interesting comparison is often the "horizontal" comparison that analyzes similar go-to-market strategies. For instance, we can compare various "freemium" strategies—providing free products to seed a market and then upselling feature-rich versions. A thought-leadership push via webinars and whitepapers combined with an inside sales model to drive opportunities to Close provides a number of metrics along the way that we can compare to similar revenue strategies. A tradeshow and field sales model should be compared with similar models from other organizations that pursue a similar path.

With best-in-class benchmarking within the same horizontal go-to-market strategy, be sure to gain clarity on where, exactly, each step should best be compared. For example, in comparing two strategies that offer a free trial, who are the users? Are they the people who registered for, downloaded, installed, or first used the software? Without clarity on these definitions, it can be difficult to draw accurate conclusions about performance.

Vertical Comparisons

Horizontal comparisons struggle to identify whether the strategy is optimal. For example, an organization may have the best and most optimized go-to-market strategy that leverages tradeshows and a field sales force, but it doesn't tell us whether a shift to webinars and an inside sales model could be even more effective.

To do that, we should create best-in-class benchmarks within the same industry. However, since this is, by definition, an attempt to look at differentiated go-to-market strategies across companies in the same industry, the metrics we assess should be as abstract from the implementation details as possible. That means using very high-level metrics such as traffic, inquiries, MQLs, SALs, and close rates—with careful observation of growth rates for each metric.

Individual differences in interim metrics—such as the number of MQLs—should be viewed in light of the metrics that precede and follow them in the buying process. If one company produces more MQLs but suffers from a lower Close rate, it may mean that the alternate approach of fewer, higher-quality MQLs performs more optimally and should be considered.

Audience Comparisons

It's also a good idea to compare your effectiveness with various audiences. Selling a multimillion-dollar offering to C-level audiences is a very different challenge than selling large volumes of a low-priced solution to individuals. As you compare various benchmarks, look at metrics such as the speed and shape of the sales pipeline, average deal sizes, staffing ratios between field sales and inside sales, and marketing mixes. From these metrics, we can make a fairer assessment of whether the audience is capable and motivated to purchase at a given size and speed.

Comparison Benchmarks

Detailed benchmarks for each of these categories are beyond the scope of this book, and will change rapidly. For that reason, a Web resource has been created to enable the sharing and analysis of benchmark data across many of the best revenue organizations in existence. As you build your revenue engine, use these peer benchmarks to ensure your revenue engine performance is on par with best organizations in your industry that target similar audiences, or share the same go-to-market strategy.

The revenue engine benchmark site can be found at http://bit.ly/REBenchmarks.

NINE

OPTIMIZE: MAKE THE TOUGH DECISIONS

OPTIMIZING REVENUE PERFORMANCE

Visibility alone can certainly motivate teams to move revenue performance in the right direction, but when executives are armed with the right data, we can significantly shift strategy and focus to drive revenue growth. That means we must make tough decisions to cut certain efforts while doubling others to drive more revenue. It can be as simple as shifting budget from one type of marketing campaign to another, as broad as moving resources from sales headcount into awareness campaigns, or as complex as cutting the marketing budget to fund objection-handling training or materials.

REDEFINING BRAND

A brand is the collective set of impressions, perceptions, and experiences we have about a specific company or product. Maintaining the brand and its reputation/ promise has been a key role for marketing. Historically, this has meant outbound messaging, sponsorships, and broad-based advertising. However, as the ways we create and communicate messages continues to evolve, our approach to managing the brand must as well. The ways brands affect the revenue engine, how they are measured, and how they can be maintained have been fundamentally transformed by the revolutionary changes in how buyers access information.

One radical change in brand management—only in its early stages, but already having major repercussions across many industries—is the way brand messaging is controlled. Historically, when mass distribution of messages was expensive, the only organizations with the motivation and ability to incur those costs were either participating in an industry or publishing media in the space.

As discussed earlier, the cost of mass communication has been reduced to zero. This affects not just marketers, obviously, but also buyers, so there are many more participants in any conversation. Customers, industry observers, various interest groups, and just about anyone with an opinion to share can now comment on a company, a product, a service experience, the treatment

of employees, or the environmental impact of a manufacturing process. Now, companies no longer control
not just the content of the conversation, but the topics of
conversation as well.

However, this lack of control in no way decreases the impact of a brand on the purchase process. Buyers' natural
impressions and perceptions of a market space, company, or solution greatly affect their likelihood of engaging
or moving through a buying process.

Effect of Brand on the Buying Process

At each stage of the buying process, a negative brand
perception reduces the chance of your marketing messages changing a prospect's perspective on the market
or showing the opportunities to improve that you offer
their business.

Awareness/Education

The relevance of various industry categories can easily
suffer from perception conflicts. If a prospect incor-
rectly believes a solution category offers nothing for her
industry, is overhyped, or is only applicable to certain
businesses, she will be less likely to pay attention to a
message that talks about the solution category. This preconceived notion of an industry or market space makes
it difficult to engage, because the potential buyer is likely
to reflexively ignore any messages regarding the market
space.

Investigation

A preconceived negative impression of your company can quickly prevent prospects from objectively considering your solutions. If the solutions have a negative brand image on key aspects, the buyer may not even read further and allow this impression to change. A successful effort in either natural or paid search, for example, is negated when a prospective buyer fails to click on the link because of a preconceived negative impression.

Validation

It's often difficult to directly evaluate many decision criteria. Often, aspects of a decision such as reliability, total cost, support levels, and robustness are evaluated as much on reputation and brand perception as they are through direct evaluation. Once a buying process reaches this stage and a prospect's perceptions have hardened, it can be difficult to change his impressions.

Management of Brand, Management of Awareness

As you can see, our ways of thinking about and managing the brand correspond directly to how we think about and manage awareness. The same concepts of reputation and unaided impressions of the company and its solutions apply equally. The main difference, however, is that we now have much more than advertising (a passive discovery mechanism) at our disposal to guide the brand.

To manage a brand today, we first must expand our view of the brand to include this full spectrum of prospect impressions. The following questions, which your prospects may be asking themselves, represent various perceptions (or misperceptions) of your brand:

- What companies have solutions to this problem?

- Which solution provider has better service?

- Which product is best in my industry or for my company size?

- Which product is the "cheap and cheerful" of the industry? Which is "robust and full-featured"?

- Which product is the most or least expensive?

- What are the key factors in deciding on a solution to this problem?

- Which company will be innovating more as we move forward?

- Which solution is more reliable? More stable? More scalable?

Whether you know it or not, your industry, company, and product have reputations, either good or bad, that shade the answers to each of these questions. These natural, unaided perceptions and preconceived ideas guide many buyer decisions. However, very few of the perceptions in the market are well-addressed by traditional investments such as logos, taglines, and naming. To manage these perceptions, we must assume a much broader role in understanding where the perceptions come from, how they are formed, how they are shared, and how to address them.

Service and Brand

One of the most interesting forces shaping brand management over the past few years has been social media. A number of forward-thinking organizations have realized that many brand-perception topics that are important to a buyer's experience could be resolved by providing the best possible product experience and then enabling and supporting word of mouth to build awareness of that message.

One of the best ways of identifying potential problems and issues that might affect any of these aspects of reputation is to monitor the discussions happening in social media. Perceptions, rants, issues, and challenges all surface via blog posts, comments on Twitter, Facebook status updates, or group discussions and conversations. When we identify these opportunities, the service team can *proactively* reach out to the affected person and attempt to resolve the issue.

This proactive resolution accomplishes three things. First, it removes a negative brand sentiment from the market by resolving that individual's issue. Second, it improves brand sentiment through the positive experience of having an issue proactively resolved. Many studies have shown that a negative experience, well resolved, can result in a more positive overall sentiment than not having any issue at all. Third, and perhaps most importantly, this public resolution of an issue resolution displays to a broader and observant audience that your brand provides excellent service.

Proactive Service, Reactive Service, and Brand

An interesting challenge arises, however. The problems typically discussed within the social media realm are much broader than those typically seen by a service help desk. That's because the threshold for calling a help desk is much higher than the threshold for complaining in social media. The difference comes down to three dimensions. Calls to a support center are generally:

- **Definable:** A discrete problem can be identified, discussed, and either resolved or not resolved.

- **Significant:** It's enough of a problem that a person picked up a phone, waited in a call queue, and brought it to your attention.

- **Solvable:** It's a problem for which one can generally visualize a defined, near-term solution.

If the problem is beyond these criteria, dissatisfied users will likely not bother phoning support because there is no reasonable expectation that the problem could be communicated and resolved.

Given these criteria, which one could call the *"something went wrong"* set of problems, businesses calculate the number of staff required for support centers. Rarely do support teams find themselves lacking work, and they are often very strapped for resources, as we manage the budgets for the call centers to maximize utilization and minimize costs.

However, if you look at the set of problems that might surface in social media, you see that these three criteria are not met.

- **Definable:** A complaint can surface without being discrete, or naturally resolvable. General dissatisfaction with airline flight delays is an example.

- **Significant:** A negative comment about a company or its products requires less effort than calling a service center, so the bar of significance is much lower.

- **Solvable:** Many problems discussed in social media are not problems that can be discretely solved in the same way that a service center can resolve many technical issues. Instead, complaints about a product's aesthetics, a company's employment policies, or previous wait times may surface.

This does not in any way suggest that these are not **important** problems, just that they are a much bigger universe of problems than the problems that make their way to today's call centers. This is the *"something failed to go right"* set of problems.

Figure 9.1 – Problem Types

We must staff our service teams to proactively reach out to the "something failed to go right" problems, rather than reactively respond to inbound "something went wrong" problems. Of course, we must staff to deal with many more problems—and this investment must be thought of in a different light. To justify investing a larger amount of resources in an area that has historically been seen as a cost center, we must look at revenue gains that are achievable with an overall improvement in brand perception.

The benefit of the communication efficiencies of today is that good reputations can and will travel almost as widely and quickly as bad reputations do. This means an investment in the actual product experience is as effective—or more- than an investment in marketing to broadly influence brand perception.

OPTIMIZING DISCOVERY

Content Marketing is the Foundation

Whether it's posted to a blog, e-mailed to an audience being nurtured, shared on social media platforms, or found via search, when it comes to being discovered by today's buyers, there's no substitute for great content. Before you implement your efforts to optimize discovery, you need to ensure a steady flow of high-quality content.

This paramount need is driven by the fundamental shift in control of the buying process. As buyers seek information—either actively via search or through the market influencers they follow—they have specific questions to answer and perspectives they hope to gain. This is the fundamental driver behind the growth in the number of words per search phrase—buyers are digging deeper and seeking more precise information. As marketers, we must have that information on hand if we hope to have it discovered by the buyer.

So what's the right process for creating this needed content? Some approaches include identifying and cultivating passionate subject matter experts inside the organization, converting internal content into public assets, or building a team of "internal publishers." Look at sales RFPs, support notes, and sales-engineering conversations for topic ideas. If prospects are seeking information in any of these forums, chances are those topics will also be sought via search or through an influencer network.

The Information Concierge

In most cases, the search engine's role is to have this information discovered. However, there is another role in the revenue process that is emerging: the "information concierge." This role bridges the gap between prospects and our valuable content. In many ways, this is what people strive to do in social media: discover conversations that relate to topics that interest them and share data, perspectives, anecdotes, and frameworks with those people in the conversations.

But isn't that what search does? Yes and no. We're all aware that Google and Bing have unprecedented power to find information. They're the main drivers of traffic for many businesses, so it seems a little counterintuitive to need an information concierge. After all, it seems like an inefficient, human-based way to solve a challenge that the search engines do so much more efficiently. But there are four reasons why the information concierge is necessary—even as search engines continue to improve:

- **Clarity:** As buyers look for deeper and deeper content, they must craft extremely precise and clear search queries. If you are looking for *"measuring e-mail deliverability rates for dedicated sending IPs,"* you may or may not locate an article discussing *"monitoring e-mail sender reputations and non-delivered e-mail counts by sender address,"*—even though that's precisely what you are looking for. The information concierge, however, puts these two independent thoughts together easily and guides the prospect to the right discussion.

- **Priority:** We all know that the first page of results on Google generates nearly all the clicks. If a great article does not find its way to the top of that list of results, then, in most cases, it is not discovered by searchers. The information concierge prioritizes differently, highlighting relevant information, but doing so based on a set of viewpoints he wants to promote and share.

- **Ease:** It can sometimes be difficult to find the information you need—but simply asking a question in an active forum can yield a very quick set of detailed and valuable responses. As marketers move

Case Example

Informatica quickly realized that a bridge exists between online and offline interactions as they began a series of analyst conferences starting with one in San Francisco. An investment in power outlets, tables, and connectivity made it easy for those interested to blog or tweet about the event, and a number of analysts did so. However, by encouraging the subsequent presenters to acknowledge and engage these questions, an interesting dynamic surfaced. As presenters answered questions that had been asked online, and the answers were shared online, analysts who were not even at the conference became engaged. Analysts from Europe and the East coast of North America joined the conversation, asking their own questions. Now, many conferences later, this dynamic has been refined to the point that a three-day conference will generate 5-6000 tweets, reaching far beyond the 1300 or so people in attendance, and spreading the Informatica message to a much broader audience.

away from attempting to *sell* to buyers and toward *facilitating their buying processes*, we need to do everything we can to make that process easier.

- **Perspective:** Perhaps the most important reason for an information concierge is the occasional need to change a buyer's perspective. If they are unaware of your solution category, think about the problem in an outdated way, or attach too much weight to the wrong criteria, only an information concierge can detect this and provide a carefully crafted case for changing that perspective.

Search is an incredibly powerful, highly relevant way for buyers to obtain information, but it remains only one part of the picture. As the amount and depth of information increases, we will likely see a much clearer, more formal information concierge role emerge. Where this role sits in the modern organization is still unclear, but it embodies elements of classic sales and marketing. The information concierge works with prospects in their early buying stages, at the Awareness or Early Investigation stages. The understanding and interpretation of buyer needs is reminiscent of sales, while the ability to connect prospective buyers with relevant information at scale is similar to the role of marketing.

OPTIMIZING THE CORE—FOCUSING ON THE MARKETING DATABASE

While awareness efforts are crucial to driving new interest, and nurturing efforts ultimately convert prospective buyers into MQLs, the marketing database holds the key to the successful transition between these two efforts. Optimizing both the data entering the database and the behavior that data can guide are key foundations to excellent revenue engine performance.

Optimizing Web Forms

Data first enters the database most frequently via Web forms—and that makes Web form performance crucial to the overall performance of the revenue engine. There are four main indicators of success with Web forms:

- **Submission Rate**—How many people who viewed the form actually submitted it?

- **Submission Profile**—Measured by A, B, C, and D fit profiles, this indicates the quality of the prospect

- **Data Quality**—The completeness and consistency of the data provided by inquirer is an important indicator of the ability to engage.

- **Data Quantity**—The number of fields that are provided by each inquirer indicates the breadth of insight provided into each prospect.

However, there are also a number of levers that a savvy revenue professional can use to optimize the quantity, quality, and amount of data they acquire from their Web forms. Depending on the desired outcome, we can alter the following characteristics to optimize the outcomes:

- **Number of Fields**—The general rule is that the more fields you request, the lower the submission rate. Although that's not *always* the case, fewer fields is usually a good goal. Some of the data you request may, in fact, be available from other sources in a more accurate and fast manner. Ask yourself: is that field truly needed or could you eliminate it and/or obtain that data some other way?

- **Field Formats and Entry Style**—We must also consider the format of the field. Should it be

Case Example

SolarWinds viewed the hands-on experience of their licensed products through a free trial as the most important aspect of buyer education and engagement. This approach guided many of their philosophies. In designing the registration form, for example, that a buyer had to fill out to download a free trial of a product, the number of fields was pared to a minimum. Only the basics of location were requested, in order to guide the lead routing process. The view was that the experience with the tool itself was a more important part of the buyer's ultimate engagement behavior with SolarWinds so hurdles between the buyer and that experience should be eliminated.

free-form or drop-down? Free-form allows a lot of user flexibility, but data will be highly varied. How is the field represented on the form? Are you asking a user to type in a location or select it on a map? Are fields auto-populated or left blank? Each of these choices affect the probability of an accurate and correct submission.

- **Progressive Profiling**—Each form is worth analyzing, but also be sure to analyze the relationships among your various forms when a visitor accesses many pieces of information over a sequence of visits. Are you needlessly asking for the same information each time? Do you remember their first visit? Do you ask for information progressively—adding to their profile over time and only asking for small increments of information each time? Progressive profiling over multiple visits can provide as much improvement as any individual improvement.

Data as an Early Guide to Strategic Segments

Many of the planning and benchmarking efforts in this book can be valuable for optimizing and expanding the revenue engine in market segments where some historical data exists. For instance, conversion rates, funnel volumes, and timeframes can be benchmarked against one another to fine-tune performance. However, occasionally, we need to target a segment of the market where there is no history of revenue performance.

These new strategic segments can be risky investments so the ability to quickly ascertain performance and tune messaging is vital. Top-performing revenue teams often look directly at the marketing database for early indicators of needed optimizations.

The first area to analyze is the fit against the existing marketing database. While a marketing database may contain a comfortable number of contacts with a high level of fit in existing segments, that may not be the case for a new strategic segment. For example, if a new strategic initiative is launched to target pharmaceutical makers, a preliminary analysis of fit in that segment may show an interesting challenge. Either a common definition of executive and organization size can be used with a pharmaceutical industry filter overlaid, or a new definition of fit can be used. Either approach shows whether messaging for the new strategic segment can be brought to the existing database, or whether investments in generating net new awareness must be made to entice new individuals to engage.

The second analysis involves a high-level active/inactive profile of the relevant segment in the database. If the newly targeted strategic segment is growing in activity, that is a leading indicator that the new messages are connecting with the new target audience. If activity is not growing as we send messages to the segment, those messages are likely not connecting with the audience in that strategic segment and may need to be reviewed for message relevance

Data Completeness and Optimizing Fit

By analyzing the fit profile in the marketing database, we have a basis for determining how many individuals may ultimately become purchasers—which is an essential baseline. Without individuals who fit well, it's unlikely any marketing efforts will generate well-qualified leads. However, this analysis relies on the underlying data.

Lead-scoring algorithms that determine fit can look at fields such as Industry, Revenue, Title, and Geography to predict whether an individual might buy in the future. If this data is absent, a scoring algorithm can only reasonably assume that the individual is not a fit. When optimizing the lead flow from the marketing database, we need to correctly understand the number of individuals within each fit level. To approximate the change in the

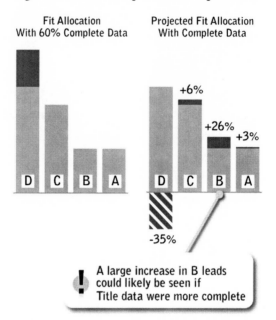

Figure 9.2 – **Data Completeness to Optimize Fit**

marketing database with complete data, let's do the following exercise:

- For individuals who have completed all of the important fields, determine the typical breakdown of values for each field.

- For those with missing data in any given field, assume that if data was present it would follow the typical distribution.

- Use this assumption to recalculate fit values of A, B, C, or D.

This approximates what the marketing database would look like in terms of fit if the data within it was complete. From this exercise, you can see which fields would be extremely valuable to populate fully. If a field is low in completeness, but would have a significant effect on fit, it may be worth using techniques like progressive profiling to guide more people to complete that field.

OPTIMIZING MARKETING INVESTMENTS

Tactical Optimization

A commonly discussed, but less commonly used, technique for tactical optimization is simple A/B testing. While A/B testing can be used in a variety of scenarios, it is best for situations that share the following four characteristics:

- **Volume:** We need a high volume of data to test—ideally at least a few thousand records.

- **Test Variable:** To avoid intermingling of effects, the test variable should be isolated and changed without any effect on the other components of the campaign.

- **Result Measurement:** We should be able to objectively measure the result clearly.

- **Timeframe:** The time between test and measurement should be short to allow the results to affect the marketing campaign in question—ideally no more than a few days.

For this reason, A/B tests are excellent for refining such elements as ad copy (such as a search or a banner ad), the subject line, images, call to action of an e-mail—or even the number of fields on a Web form. However, for many marketing efforts, such as webinars, tradeshows, or regional events, there is no opportunity to optimize anything more than small components of the effort. For these marketing efforts, a broader framework is needed.

Revenue Influence as a Guide

As we have seen in previous chapters, each individual campaign can be benchmarked against its peers and analyzed to see its effect on buyers' movements through the funnel. However, we also need high-level views to optimize the overall revenue engine. While there are many factors involved in guiding a prospect, it's particularly helpful for us to know what campaigns were influential across a broad range of buyers—so that we can amplify those efforts and effects.

Let's create this view by connecting each campaign to the revenue it influenced. Any successful touch point that influences an individual buyer—such as a click on an e-mail, a visit to a tradeshow booth, or a view of a whitepaper –counts as influencing the resulting revenue. At this high level, there's no need to assess percentages or allocate revenue to each campaign that influenced it. Instead, this is simply a view of what campaigns had *any* effect on the deals that resulted.

Viewed in this way, a number of marketing insights become visible. First, this holistic view may reveal insights not otherwise obvious in terms of how buyers formulate opinions. For instance, a webinar might have been designed to generate early-stage leads but failed to deliver. Nonetheless, the webinar appears to be a strong performer in our "influenced revenue" analysis. Therefore, we should revisit our expectations and assessment of that webinar. Perhaps it catered to a critical buyer role in a way that few other campaigns did. Or perhaps it positioned a certain value proposition in a way that accelerated deals better than any other communication.

This view of influenced revenue provides a starting point for deeper analysis of what actually guides prospect behaviors in a way that treats the buying process holistically.

Figure 9.3 – **Influenced Revenue as a Guide**

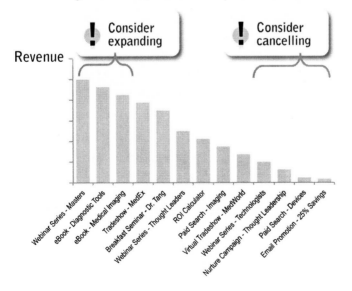

Looking Forward into the Pipeline

When optimizing marketing campaigns or choosing among alternatives, the most common output to be analyzed is the closest to what is being driven. If a broad advertising campaign mostly drives awareness, measures of traffic are most often looked at. If a search campaign drives new inquiries via a download form for a web asset, these inquiries likely are the most common output to be analyzed.

This is effective for making short-term tradeoffs among campaign alternatives, but it assumes that we should treat all buyers at a particular stage in the same way. While that's a necessary and practical assumption, a deeper view of the buying process can fine tune the overall performance of a revenue engine. For example, if a campaign drives MQLs, consider looking at the *performance* of those MQLs as they progress through the various stages of the sales cycle to understand if any performance gaps exist.

As can be seen in the following chart, the MQLs created by the webinar campaign tend to move to the needs analysis stage very effectively, compared to the overall average for MQLs, but then they get stuck and are unable to progress. This may indicate that their level of interest is not being fully assessed.

While many other factors influence whether these MQLs progress through the funnel, any trends in either

Figure 9.4 – **Optimizing by Comparing Pipeline Performance**

		Webinar Campaign			MQL Average		Variance	
		Size	Age	CR%	Age	CR%	Speed	CR%
MQLs		100						
SALs		70		70%		60%		10%
SQOs [e]	Needs Analysis	60	50	86%	30	50%	67%	36%
[d]	Solution Presentation	16	40	27%	40	50%	0%	-23%
[c]	Solution Proposal	8	50	50%	50	50%	0%	0%
[b]	Commitment /Negotiation	4	60	50%	60	40%	0%	10%
[a]	Closed Won	2	70	50%	70	40%	0%	10%

CR = Conversion Rate

! More moving to Stage **e**, BUT challenges moving to Stage **d**

conversion rates or conversion speeds should be investigated. If there is a conspicuous issue, it may indicate one or more of the following challenges:

- **Buying Committee:** If deals get stuck at stages that require the actions, consent, or involvement of a broader buying committee, we may need either broader marketing messaging earlier in the process or more buying-committee-level qualification criteria in the lead scoring algorithm that defines an MQL.

- **Messaging:** If deals stagnate in the early stages, there may be a disconnect between the messages that buyers hear and what they actually discover as they interact with sales.

- **Territory:** A geographic or industry territory may not have sufficient referenceabilty or strong enough messaging. In this territory, you may need a deeper level of MQL qualification to ensure strong sales engagement.

Each challenge can be quickly identified and solved via messaging, targeting, or qualification changes, but we must create a view of the lifecycle for each inquiry or MQL to bring this level of insight forward.

Optimizing the MQL Definition

The next challenge is to optimize the MQL definition. With leads scored on the basis of fit, from A to D, and engagement, from 1 to 4, we can create our grid of lead quality. The best of these—that is, those closest to the A1 definition—are MQLs and passed to sales for deeper engagement. Within all of these MQLs, a quality gradation exists, which is an opportunity to optimize the time and efforts of the sales team.

To visualize how to best define the MQL, chart the progress of MQL leads by quality as they progress through the sales pipeline. If your scoring is meaningful, you should see more higher-quality A1 MQLs move through the pipeline, while lower-quality B3 and C2 leads, on average, shake out of the pipeline or proceed more slowly.

Over time, this quality shakeout pattern will show where changes are needed (if any) in the MQL definition to maximize sales efficiency. If a given quality ranking generally does not make it through the pipeline, exclude it from your future MQL definition.

Figure 9.5 – **Lead Quality Shake-out**

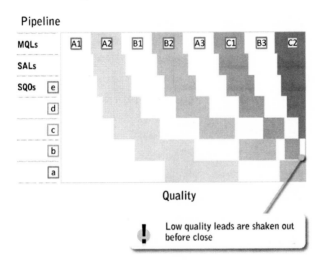

MAXIMIZING LEAD FLOW

The next opportunity to optimize your revenue performance management lies in the handoff from marketing to sales after the lead is deemed an MQL. This handoff is very critical because it is the point when the buyer moves from a more passive approach to an actively managed sales process. It's the transition from mainly rules-based nurturing and scoring to a sales process managed by people. The transition between these two separate departments—sales and marketing—requires a careful handoff process.

Optimizing Lead Hand-off

The handoff from marketing to sales indicates that a buyer has been detected who are of sufficiently good fit and sufficiently strong engagement that a conversation with a salesperson will likely be worthwhile for them and for the organization. A successful handoff is when a sales qualified opportunity (SQO) has been created. This validates the correctness of the MQL assessment/definition and indicates that the salesperson was able to connect with the prospect, and that in the initial conversation, it appeared that an opportunity existed.

Optimizing this area of the process depends on recognizing that each salesperson only has a defined capacity to make calls in a given period of time. If too many leads are received, the salesperson must spend less time understanding how best to connect with the buyer and what their areas of interest are or the speed

Figure 9.6 – **Lead Capacity**

	MQLs		Capacity	SQOs	SQO/MQL	
John	200	■	100	75	38%	■
Anya	180	■	100	70	39%	■
Susan	30	▏	100	22	73%	■
Raj	45	▏	100	30	67%	■
Total	455		400	197	43%	

! Too many MQLs leads to a lower than average conversion rate

Case Example

With more than 2 years of historical benchmark data on lead flow and sales conversions, the Platts team is able to calculate the required volume of leads each rep will need in order to make their quota. Marketing efforts are catered to this capacity and carefully adjusted in order to ensure a steady predictable growth in revenue many quarters out. When, for example, the lead pipeline in Eastern Europe was found to be significantly lower than it needed to be, the field marketing team confirmed that indeed leads and opportunities were in short supply there. They worked quickly with sales to help remedy this issue by taking advantage of a recent regulatory change in a number of Eastern European countries was causing concern among buyers and had become top of mind. Shifting both outbound email and inbound search campaigns to address this top of mind issue, the Platts team was able to restock the lead pipeline and avert a revenue dip a few quarters out.

and frequency of follow-up will drop due to insufficient time. Either of these outcomes significantly reduces the likelihood of a successful connection, which means the effectiveness of the lead handoff process suffers.

At the opposite end of the spectrum, of course, too few leads means the salesperson must do a significant amount of prospecting. While some level of direct prospecting is often a very good thing, it is not always an efficient way to identify new opportunities. To maximize revenue engine efficiency, each salesperson should receive a lead flow that keeps them at or near their capacity to process leads.

Approximating this capacity is quite straightforward. The quota of each salesperson, divided by average deal size, provides the number of deals in a quarter. Looking at this number and the team's average conversion rate from SQO to close tells us the number of opportunities that must be worked to create the needed number of deals. If the average MQL to SQO conversion rate is then factored in, we have a good estimate of the capacity of each salesperson to consume MQLs per quarter.

If there are too many MQLs and the sales team shows the resulting inefficiencies, we should reduce the number of MQLs by increasing our qualification standards. We would pass a smaller number of better MQLs to sales, and the resulting SQO conversion rate will improve dramatically.

Operational Challenges in Marketing/Sales Alignment

This view, however, is often seen over the course of an entire quarter. While instructive and useful for balancing lead flow, it overlooks the shorter-time-frame challenges. Sales and marketing are very different organizations. Even in forward-leaning organizations that invest heavily in prospects throughout their buying process, marketing is often still organized around campaigns or events. On the other side, sales, being a people discipline, is organized around salespeople's time.

> **Case Example**
>
> SolarWinds' early success, and the products they offered had meant a wealth of inquiries. In the early days, 1000s of inquiries per week were being passed to a very small sales team. This resulted in each salesperson picking which inquiries they would follow up with, and leaving the rest to be unaddressed. Each salesperson did this differently, and each based their selection on a guess as to what made a good lead, whether it was their company, their title, or how they had engaged. In order to optimize this lead follow-up process, the SolarWinds team analyzed the buying process to see what activities, demographics, firmographics, or sources correlated with eventually becoming a paying customer. Those web visitors who opted in to download a 30 day trial of the licensed version of the software were deemed to be a 'sales qualified lead' and the sales team focused their efforts on those leads.
>
> SolarWinds carefully balanced the investments they made in marketing and sales. Instead of operating separately, the marketing and sales teams orchestrated their efforts to ensure the efficient distribution of leads. Sales and marketing, working together, designed a flexible structure that enabled sales to respond to demand as it came in.

These operational styles become very apparent when your sales and marketing teams align very closely around the lead handoff process. As this process becomes tighter, the natural propensity of marketing to run campaigns or events that generate point-in-time spikes in leads, can overwhelm the sales team's ability to

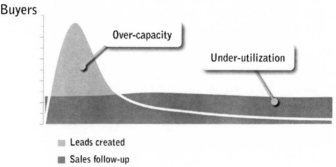

Figure 9.7 – **Operational Alignment of Sales and Marketing**

quickly follow up on those leads, which is restricted to the number of salespeople on the team and the number of hours in a day.

It is usually very difficult to make instantaneous adjustments in the number of salespeople available to call hot leads, and the number of hours in a day, of course, doesn't change. This leaves a challenging disconnect: If a marketing campaign generates a spike of MQLs on a Monday, for example, and those leads are passed to sales, it will swamp the sales team's ability to respond. Calls will spill over into Tuesday and Wednesday, where the sales team will face declining success rates because of the elapsed time, and by Thursday, the sales team will be out of leads.

A far better solution is to "throttle" marketing campaigns to produce a steadier stream of leads flowing to sales. Not all campaigns can be throttled—but many can. For example, a lead-generating e-mail campaign can be split it into five equal amounts and "dropped" over the course of five days—that's better than sending to everyone simultaneously. This prevents the sales team from being overwhelmed with leads on day one and also increases the successful connections they make. And those connections will keep them busier with the same number of leads.

The need to optimize this handoff process is a sign that sales/marketing alignment is growing much stronger. As it does, adjusting the operational styles of marketing to meet the realities of salespeople on phones will improve the SQO/MQL conversion rate.

Looking at Issues

If we discover issues in lead handoff outside these two optimization approaches, there may be misalignment in lead-scoring and MQL definition. Continual changes in market dynamics, buyer sophistication, product offerings, or competitive strategies mean this definition must be continually revisited—as frequently as every six weeks for a new process or every quarter for more stable processes.

To understand how well our revenue engine delivers MQLs that convert into SQOs, let's look at two views of the process.

Percentage of Leads that Close

First let's get a long-term view of our MQLs—for a period that is two or three times the length of the average sales cycle. What percentage of these MQLs close? In many organizations, there are also lead sources that are outside of this marketing stream. What are the close rates for those leads? This yields a good baseline for how effective our scoring model is in identifying quality leads.

Percentage of Deals from Qualified Leads

The opposite view looks at all deals that close in a time period and analyzes what percentage were MQLs. We can look at its total revenue (if there is a broad range of deal sizes). This percentage helps us understand whether the lead flow from marketing's nurturing processes has a significant impact on overall sales performance and pipeline.

These two views indicate whether our MQL definition truly defines a lead that converts into revenue. A breakdown in this handoff process is an opportunity to address that definition and realign sales and marketing.

"Cherry-picking" of leads from the marketing funnel is a great example of a process breakdown that can give us valuable insights. If the sales team is permitted to pull leads from the marketing funnel before they reach the MQL threshold, it serves as an early warning that the agreed-upon criteria for lead qualification and the overall optimization of lead volume are not ideal.

GROWING SALES

The final optimization point is the sales process. When buyers engage with content, become interested, get defined as qualified, and successfully connect with the appropriate salesperson, we want to ensure a transaction successfully concludes. In today's buyer-led world, however, there are numerous opportunities to improve this aspect of the revenue engine based on new insights and new ways in which relationships develop. While many sales skills and disciplines remain unchanged, the best revenue organizations see new opportunities to optimize beyond what was previously possible.

Inside Sales *vs.* Outside Sales

One key role that can help drive explosive growth is the inside sales rep. The online world is redefining how people develop and maintain trust—and that's leading many organizations to rethink how they invest in sales teams. New interactions and engagement online are replacing how trust was traditionally built: face to face. As this happens, the emphasis on in-person interaction and the need to be "in the field" decreases. While the discipline of field sales itself is unlikely to disappear any time soon, the economic threshold for face-to-face interaction is moving dramatically.

Historically, inside sales teams generally closed deals with an average selling price (ASP) of less than $20,000. Today, these teams now close deals at much larger ASPs. Some organizations are seeing effective inside sales for ASPs of up to $100,000. Inside sales teams develop this effectiveness by building trusted relationships through online interactions and presence in communities, understanding key players in buying committees through LinkedIn and other online tools, and relying on a company reputation that is kept honest by the openness with which knowledge is shared.

Although face-to-face interactions will continue to remain a powerful way to build trust—especially for larger transactions—the efficiencies and cost-effectiveness of the inside sales model make it very compelling for smaller transactions. This efficiency, combined with a growing ability to build trust through means other than eye contact, are moving inside sales in many organizations from small transactions to much larger transactions. This trend is certain to grow as communication tools and trust-building approaches continue to tip the balance in favor of the inside sales model.

Optimizing Based on Sales Insights

While the numbers and conversion rates for each stage of the revenue engine show us what can be optimized, the insights of sales professionals are often of equal or greater value. The experience, intuition, and current deal activities give sales professionals a unique lens with which to view the online activities of prospective buyers.

By providing sales with this view of buyer activity at the individual, team, and territory level, we not only enable sales professionals to be significantly more effective, we also open a channel of communication with marketing that supports the entire communication process from early stage awareness through to the closing of a deal.

Insights into Individual Buyers

Each action that a prospect takes on the website or in response to a marketing campaign sheds light on them as a buyer. Each e-mail that is opened or clicked on, each website visit, each Google search, or each form submission helps us understand their digital body language. Are they interested? What are they interested in? What conversation topics engage them? Many of these insights, especially from new content, may not yet be reflected in the automated rules that are used to score and nurture leads. The best way to identify new insights into buyer behavior is to have the people on the front line use their experience and intuition to identify new buying patterns. While looking for these new patterns, individual sales professionals can move buying processes forward significantly by identifying conversation opportunities and hot buttons in individual buyer behavior.

Trends in activity, spikes of interest, and renewed interest after dormant periods are all useful indicators that internal activities at the prospect's company or market changes are driving buying activity. These are all crucial for a salesperson to know, and are best conveyed visually to allow quick insights. Experienced sales professionals

> **Case Example**
>
> Within the IT infrastructure management space, different experts focus on slightly different areas. System administrators, network engineers, storage managers, and network architects may each have slightly different problems that they work on in an IT organization. When SolarWinds designed their library of free tools, they did it with this in mind. Tools were designed to appeal to each different role. As a result, SolarWinds designed their marketing campaigns for paid product options available for those users to fit those roles. The SolarWinds online lead nurture program presented paid product options to each prospective buyer using a consumer marketing-like model of "if you liked X, you may also like Y".

armed with these insights can help us know what type of content is being viewed, or searches being performed, more accurately indicate the conversations that will interest a buyer.

Insights into Key Players in a Buying Team

By tracking the interest profile of each buyer and giving the sales team an account-level view of the activities of each person, we show sales that organization's internal dynamics. Sales can see who is most engaged, who is disengaged, and who shows signs of interest but is not currently part of the conversation. That helps sales drive deal processes within those accounts by knowing how to navigate the internal politics and unknown motivations.

In B2B buying, the person doing the bulk of the research is often not the ultimate buyer. But detailed research does indicate there is likely a buying process underway. Marketing can support their sales team quickly and easily by working with a role-based name discovery service to automatically discover the key individuals in the buyer's role within that prospect organization.

Sales professionals who have leveraged this insight in active buying processes can show marketing who within a buying team is likely to engage with what content. Trends in missing buyer roles can often be more quickly identified by front line sales professionals than by waiting for evidence of stuck deals.

Insights into Active Buying Processes Within a Territory

As a salesperson works his territory to uncover the companies that might be interested, he needs insight into which companies might be starting research due to internal business events. This can sometimes be hard to determine, but we can provide the insights to make this process easier and more efficient. The marketing team, which scores leads based on the level of buying activity, can roll up this scoring to the account level, offering a view of which key accounts within a salesperson's territory show coordinated buying activity.

We can make this insight actionable by putting it into a territory dashboard that quickly highlights active accounts that deserve heightened attention as well as any long-dormant accounts that have begun to show renewed activity. Sales success depends on devoting efforts on the right accounts. Sales teams that quickly identify the right accounts will consistently perform well.

With this insight, sales professionals can guide marketing by identifying early trends in the market, such as increasing interest from organizations in a specific vertical, or from organizations using a competitor's product. These insights help us create highly targeted marketing campaigns that capitalize on newly discovered interest—before competitors can react.

Deal Insights to Optimize Results

Deal analysis is an alternate way to deepen our understanding of how revenue flows through the revenue engine. This view of a deal allows a quick understanding of the revenue engine from the perspective of a single buying process. This "deal-backwards" view of influence shows how the buying team progressed through the buying process. This single-account analysis often provides interesting insights into what marketing assets had a greater effect than originally thought, or what buyer roles appeared to play larger or smaller roles than anticipated.

Each deal viewed in this manner shows whether the buyer's path to purchase was roughly what we anticipated. If not, we should remap the assumptions of the buying journey, as discussed in Chapter 3. Also, we can assess buying activities and how they map to the stages of the buying process to validate whether changes are needed in lead scoring.

As buyers continue to obtain more of the information they require online, and marketers facilitate this by publishing the right content, the path toward buying becomes increasingly clear.

Figure 9.8 – **Deal Insights to Optimize Results**

Deal: Acme Co	Date	Interaction	
Alan Crandon, VP Sales			
Industry Tradeshow	1/3/2010	Registered; Attended	
ROI Calculator Email	1/28/2010	Opened; Clicked; Submitted	
Case Study Email	2/15/2010	Opened; Clicked	
Sharon Connelly, Dir. Marketing			
Video Testimonial Email	1/28/2010	Opened; Clicked	
Thought Leadership Webinar	3/12/2010	Registered; Attended	
Technical Blog	3/15/2010	Visited	
Closed Won			

Stuck Deals, Content Insights

Examining the deal flow in the sales pipeline provides clear insights into how we can improve the overall revenue process. The best source is "stuck deals." Look at the average age of deals in the pipeline to identify any "clumps" of deals that stagnate at roughly the same spot—these are the deals that are significantly older than the average age.

Let's look at each stage and examine whether there are any insights to be gained from deals that are stuck in that stage:

E—Needs Analysis

Do leads from a certain source have a greater tendency to get stuck in this stage? If so, are those leads not looking at certain key market assets? Are leads that move

> **Case Example**
>
> The Platts team analyzed the speed with which deals flowed through their sales process and found some valuable insights. In one instance, a newly introduced product was found to have a higher proportion of deals stuck at the "resolution of concerns" stage in their sales process. Investigation of this anomaly quickly uncovered the fact that because it was a new product, buyers were hesitant to purchase until they had seen others make the purchase before them. Armed with this insight, the Platts team now considers case studies and video testimonials upfront in the product launch process and looks to secure recognizable reference accounts even before a new product is publicly launched.

forward typically looking at those assets? Often, a key sign that a buyer is ready for needs analysis is that they start viewing much more tactical content, indicating they have moved from conceptual interest to stronger interest in making a purchase. This trend may mean we should increase the importance of tactical content in the scoring criteria that define an MQL.

D—Solution Presentation

If deals get stuck in the solution presentation stage, we need to find out what's required to move them out of this stage. Generally, these customer proof points will center around an executive sponsor agreeing with the economic value of the solution. Look for differences in overall team engagement. For example, if stuck deals show a conspicuous absence of online research activity, the individual you are engaged with might not have the motivation or political power to promote the solution and get buy-in.

C—Solution Proposal

Deals stuck at this stage reflect an inability to make the buying committee comfortable with the overall solution proposed. Look for signs that key stakeholders are not present in these stuck deals. For example, if deals with financial services organizations get stuck more frequently, you might learn that your sales team isn't effectively engaging these prospects' security teams. Similarly, if a key executive, such as a CMO is engaged in deals that move forward, but is absent in stuck deals, you'll want to ensure that the CMO gets engaged earlier.

B—Commitment and Negotiation

Deals stuck at this final stage are the most frustrating of all because they look like wins before stalling at the last minute. Look for signs that the buying committee has not yet made the necessary emotional or economic commitment. For instance, if the buying committee is still actively accessing thought-leadership content or ROI calculators, it indicates the required level of commitment is not yet present.

Each insight translates into potentially required action from the revenue team. If your new insights show that there's content the prospect should see before moving to

Case Example

When technical IT buyers discovered SolarWinds, they next needed to understand whether SolarWinds could truly help them solve the specific problem they were tackling. To provide this insight, SolarWinds provided a full-featured 21 or 30 day free trial on every one of their products. This investment in validation ensured that the late stages of the buying process went smoothly as it was exceptionally easy for a prospective buyer to validate that the SolarWinds products would truly solve the challenge they were facing, in their environment, in an effective way. Seeing a buyer move to this stage of validation by downloading a trial version, in fact, quickly become the top indicator of buying intent.

the next stage, the marketing and sales teams must collectively ensure this content is appropriately presented to the buying team.

If the buying team has had ample opportunity to engage with this content—but hasn't done so—it's a sign that a deeper conversation in that topic area may be required. Or if you learn that a key stakeholder role has been less involved than he should be, it suggests your earlier nurture campaigns should seek out those stakeholders to raise and resolve any issues earlier.

Territory Planning

Another critical aspect of managing a sales force is careful territory planning. You can define them by geography, industry, revenue range, or in a variety of more creative ways, but the goal is always the same: to define the set of accounts that each salesperson or each sales team is permitted to pursue.

Common methodologies for finding the right balance in territories often combine company fit with current penetration. Company fit—comprised of industry, company size, revenues, and strategy—lets us approximate the anticipated spend of that organization. Share of wallet, or account penetration, shows how much of this potential spend you have currently achieved.

With these two dimensions, we can plot the companies within a territory. Each quadrant requires a different focus, and hence, often, a different type of person. High-spend, high-penetration accounts are of very high value and there is often continuous potential to develop these accounts even further with a "farmer" type of salesperson. High-spend, low-penetration accounts have great potential for a "hunter" type of salesperson who generates lots of new business. Low-spend, high penetration accounts have limited upside potential and have already been fully developed, so we should assign those accounts to an account manager. The low-spend, low-penetration quadrant is the least promising and is often not worth pursuing.

This 2x2 view of the territory allows us to allocate staff in terms of numbers and skills. The ratio of staff to accounts will vary widely by industry, but even within an industry we will see a wide range based on account

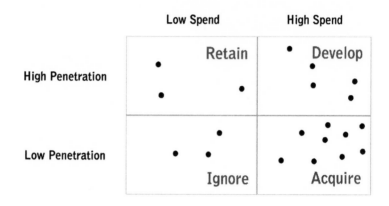

Figure 9.9 – Territory Planning

type. Acquiring accounts may require a 1:5 ratio, while developing them only necessitates a 1:20 ratio. Retaining may be as high as a 1:50 ratio in many cases. Using these staffing ratios and account breakdowns, we can develop a territory plan that balances the size and economic potential, and supports equitable compensation planning across diverse territories.

Timing Territories

While this methodology and many similar approaches let us assess the total long-term potential, they don't show when that territory is ready for a change in sales focus. This is crucial because mistiming the hiring of sales professionals is one of the most expensive mistakes a growing company can make. Deploying sales professionals in territories without active deals means there are few client scenarios that enable them to gain relevant selling experience. They are unable to refine their selling skills and struggle to succeed.

The optimum time to hire sales professionals is after you have developed an active pipeline. The salesperson can quickly gain real selling experience and augment her training and role-playing practice. That requires a view of the territory map that looks at engagement, not just fit. Active pipeline opportunities develop from accounts that are highly engaged, with or without an ideal fit. That can only be determined by examining the overall online activity of accounts within the territory.

Viewing the territory by level of engagement lets us assess when the resources should be in place. A territory showing great potential, but without much engagement, must first receive focus from the marketing team to build awareness and increase levels of engagement. A territory that's already showing high levels of engagement can be staffed with sales professionals immediately.

Figure 9.10 – **Territory Timing by Engagement**

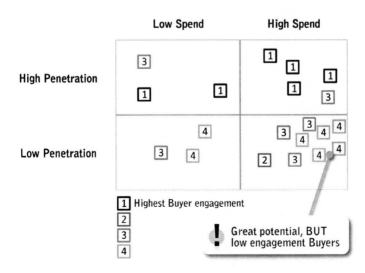

Ramping Sales Reps

These analyses generally focus on the revenue engine in a steady state, assuming a fully ramped, comfortable, and familiar sales force. Of course, that's not the case in many organizations. In many B2B sales organizations, the time to bring a salesperson up to full productivity can be as much as nine months. If there's moderate growth or moderate team turnover, this means that the efficiency of this critical, and expensive, resource is much lower than it should be.

Bringing sales professionals up to full productivity, assuming they arrive with some previous sales experience, results from three main factors:

- **Training:** The rep needs industry and company knowledge to understand the value proposition, offerings, pricing, services, and client successes that can be communicated to prospects

- **Field Experience:** She needs experience working with actual prospects in a true selling environment to crystallize and clarify the lessons learned in training.

- **Deal Pipeline:** Once this knowledge has been internalized, a successful salesperson must build a pipeline of deals, each of which can take months to close, before full quota attainment is achieved.

Marketing can significantly facilitate two of these three factors. If a new salesperson gets placed in a new geography, industry, or market segment, marketing can ensure the lead flow in that territory is maximized prior to his start. With a healthy flow of leads at the start of his tenure, the salesperson can gain field experience and build a healthy pipeline months sooner than if he started without leads. This minimizes not only ramp time, but also the likelihood of salesperson attrition due to a lack of early success.

CONTINUAL OPTIMIZATION, CONTINUAL GROWTH

Optimizing the revenue process is a continuous effort. Markets shift, buyers change, solutions evolve, and new competitors arise. What's more, improvements in some areas of the revenue engine may increase pressure in other areas as volumes grow.

The optimization tools in this chapter provide a framework for analyzing the revenue engine holistically, and making decisions in the context of their overall effects. Viewed in this way, the investments and efforts undertaken can maximize the company's ability to drive revenue in the short- and long-term.

This ability to optimize the revenue engine from beginning to end, regardless of the current delineation between marketing and sales or between siloed disciplines in each group, will differentiate high-performance revenue teams of the future.

TEN

THE REVENUE ENGINE AS STRATEGIC IMPERATIVE

Today's best-performing organizations are setting new standards in how they manage the revenue engine. For the first time, investments in both marketing and sales can be seen through the common lens of revenue. Without ignoring the complexities of lengthy B2B (or high-ticket B2C) buying cycles, these organizations create a single view of the truth that enables them to see where prospects are in their buying process, how they are moving through the buying process, and what investments can best accelerate those processes.

While revenue performance management offers immediate gains in driving more revenue with less investment, it also provides strategic advantages that extend far beyond mere revenue growth. As we enter into the second decade of the new millennium, competitive advantage accrues to those who best align all of their corporate resources around the markets, geographies, and products with the greatest potential. As the pace of technological innovation and adoption accelerates, product lifecycles shorten. Organizations that identify and time market adoption patterns perfectly will be poised to win, while organizations that are too early or too late will flounder.

STRATEGIC DECISIONS

Nothing is a truer indication of a market's readiness than its willingness to make purchases. For executives facing the difficult strategic decisions of when and where to make marketing and sales investments, a well-tuned revenue engine can provide higher-level insights into market readiness that is as vital to strategic planning as any other organizational capability.

In most organizations, executive discussions center on revenue: how to grow or protect it, where it is coming from, and how to capture it most economically. Even discussions that don't center on revenue are, of course, profoundly affected by it as well, including production and manufacturing planning, budget allocations, and service and support projections, to name just a few. For lack of better alternatives, these discussions are often based on linear growth projections based on historical averages. This approach can leave the organization unprepared for any disruptive revenue surprises—positive or negative. But, if we're armed with the insights that a well-tuned revenue engine can provide, we can shift resources, ramp or throttle production, or adjust financial plans to take advantage of these shifting market dynamics.

Market Sizing

A significant challenge in any vibrant and growing market lies in understanding its overall size at any moment in time. Investments to generate revenue only succeed to the extent that a market exists—but if buyers are not actively engaged in reading and learning about a solution space, later stage revenue investments are unlikely to pay off. However, failing to invest as a growing market heats up can translate into a lost opportunity to capture market leadership position and being relegated to a second or third place.

The challenge with market sizing, however, is that it is often based on very late-stage data. Analysts look at reported purchases and extrapolate linearly. Companies without an integrated revenue engine will look at sales cycles that are near to close and extrapolate from there. Neither approach provides much insight beyond the near term if there is a sudden up-tick or down-tick in demand.

A well-tuned revenue engine, however, gives us market size/growth insights that extend much further into the future. With historical insights into conversion rates between early-stage audience activity (such as search trends, traffic on particular areas of content, or inquiry patterns) and latter-stage activity (such as MQL creation, opportunity progress, and deal close), we can predict whether an overall market will be flat, up, or down as much as one or two years into the future.

This leading indicator lets us appropriately size our budgets, teams, and investments to capture the leading share of a hot market or be the first to reallocate resources if a market cools off.

Territory Planning

The allocation of resources to either geographic or industry territories follows a similar pattern at a smaller scale. When executives are evaluating strategic decisions for sales territory plans, field events, or verticalized messaging, they need to understand each territory's potential, both in the current timeframe and within one to three years. A well-managed revenue engine can not only identify proactive market interest using the search, traffic, and content activity indicators we've discussed. It can also assess how much of that interest is actively managed.

For buyers who are not actively engaged, we can understand a territory's likely potential based on a fit analysis of names in the marketing database. By looking at buyer roles in deals that were won, a pattern of ideal fit emerges. With this lens on buyer fit, we can analyze the marketing database to see if the right set of buyer roles, at the right companies, in the right industries exist for a given territory.

Given this two-part equation, territory efforts can be planned accordingly. If buyers are known but signs of engagement are absent, nurturing efforts are needed. If online engagement and activity exists, but buyers are unknown, we need to directly connect with buyers. If both activity and known buyers exist, we might allocate additional sales resources to the territory.

Product Mix Assessment

We can also assess expected trends in the product mix for one or two years out. By looking at search terms being used, the roles of inquiring prospects, or the content being consumed most frequently, we can see the product mix areas of interest. While not rigorously predictive, this can be the equivalent of a broad online focus group, giving strong leading indicators of upcoming changes in the product mix that will be purchased.

By understanding the expected product purchase mix, we can more accurately assess future profitability, make smarter logistics or manufacturing decisions, and target our product development efforts to the best product lines.

As early-stage buyers transition into inquiries and MQLs, this mix assessment can be fine-tuned to be more accurate, but with a shorter time horizon. Over time, this fine tuning can also help with more precisely using the early-stage indicators to predict future product mixes more accurately.

Pipeline Flow and Stuck Deals

There are only two factors to indicate the overall potential revenue of a sales team's pipeline: its size and its speed. Too often, we focus on size to the exclusion of speed, because it's easier to measure. However, both factors have an identical effect on total revenue, and speed is the factor that is much more affected by your actions (or inactions).

An executive team focused on pipeline speed and days leads outstanding (DLOs) quickly identifies issues before they have a material effect on results. With a well-built revenue engine, the organization enjoys very good insights into buyer roles and messages that are critical for a deal to close. When a trend of stuck deals is identified, it represents an opportunity to realign buyer roles and messages.

If a new competitor successfully changes the playing field or lodges an objection in the mind of prospects, deals then tend to get consistently stuck at a particular spot. If a certain industry needs the approval or buy-in of a particular role, then deals in that industry become stuck unless we identify and nurture this role accordingly.

By focusing on speed in addition to overall pipeline size, we can increase total revenue and proactively identify and resolve potentially damaging issues. Organizations without a fully instrumented revenue engine are often unable to properly measure pipeline speed or build strategies for revenue growth and optimization.

Budget Planning

A significant percentage of any annual budget is allocated to driving revenue. However, within the disciplines of marketing and sales, there is often very little science to allocating budgetary dollars. Rather than allocation based on market need, most allocations are based on historical averages, industry norms, or executive negotiations.

However, with the revenue engine's single view of the truth, this debate concludes quickly and appropriately. By first understanding where buyers fall within the full buying cycle—from early stage awareness through Close—and analyzing the historical and expected conversion rates, budgets can be allocated based on known pipeline challenges, and allocated to initiatives likely to have the most positive impact.

Campaign Planning

Within the marketing organization itself, a similar dynamic takes place: a large amount of discretionary spending goes into a wide variety of marketing campaigns. Without insights into prospect behavior or an understanding how it fits into an end-to-end buying process, these campaign efforts tend to be spread liberally among all aspects of the buying process—from early-stage awareness to deeper investigation and final solution validation.

However, that isn't always the right way. An analytical understanding of the revenue engine might show how to significantly reallocate investments. If a revenue performance challenge is related to how economic buyers compare your solutions to a competitor's, you can address that with proper marketing messaging. Similarly, if the sales team is overcapacity with leads, you would reduce lead-generation in favor of efforts to increase the qualification of MQLs or increase the Close rate for leads that are sent over to sales.

Sales Quota Planning

At the final stage of the revenue process, where the sales team is engaged with buyers, it may seem that the interactions are too individualized to merit or withstand the same level of numerical analysis. Nothing could be further from the truth. A sales team is nearly always governed by a careful structure of territories and quotas. Sales team performance is measured and analyzed against quotas for each team.

A revenue engine that provides an understanding of buyers at every stage can provide a much more accurate method of territory planning than any other approach. For instance, recognizing which territories have a high level of active interest but a low level of market penetration, and which have low levels of interest or complete market penetration, lets us allocate both the type of sales professional and his associated quota in the most effective manner.

Similarly, the hiring plan for new sales reps in each territory often receives strategic attention—for a very good reason: In most organizations, these are among the most expensive hires, and can take many months or many quarters to reach full productivity. The hiring sequence should be one of the more carefully planned hiring strategies at most organizations.

Recognizing when buyers in a specific territory are ready to engage with sales and when a territory would be better served by marketing awareness efforts lets us time sales hires and appropriately optimize their associated ramps.

Messaging Changes

In many instances, a market's evolution requires a change in messaging. As this happens, buyers shift from needing education on why a solution category is different to why one solution within the category is different than other options. Understanding when to make this strategic messaging shift is often difficult. If it's done too early, buyers will not understand the rationale for the solution category. If the shift to a more competitive stance is done too late, you will still be investing in educating a market that your competitors will be selling products directly into.

A well-crafted revenue engine presents an excellent picture of this transition. As the market shifts, the search terms buyers use and the content they find compelling shifts as well. By carefully monitoring overall search terms used and the most popular content, and correlating those trends with the number of inquiries and MQLs created, this shift can be proactively detected and addressed.

By recognizing this shift before competitors do, organizations can retrain their sales team in time to capitalize on the market's move and quickly achieve market dominance against other organizations that are slower to react.

New Go-To-Market Strategies

As markets mature and the messaging moves from evangelical to mainstream, we can also identify new market opportunities and go-to-market strategies. The well-instrumented revenue engine provides insights into unique buying roles, and can even identify new roles with new needs. For instance, a more junior role than typical might begin seeking a solution that historically had formed a small piece of a more comprehensive offering. If this trend is observed more broadly, the company might, for instance, repackage or create a new offering targeted at the emerging market niche.

As technology changes both what is possible and how buyers learn and purchase, new changes in go-to-market and product strategy become increasingly frequent.

Companies that quickly identify and act decisively on opportunities will have a significant edge.

THE FUTURE OF THE REVENUE ENGINE

We have reached an inflection point in the way organizations think about generating revenue. Rather than view revenue as a difficult-to-predict outcome resulting from the efforts of multiple groups in two or more functions, leading businesses are now thinking of a single revenue engine that spans both marketing and sales. Rather than simply blasting outbound campaigns to a particular demographic or firmographic segment with a targeted message and hoping a small percentage convert to buyers, we can now learn how buyers buy, where they gather the information that guides their perspectives, and strive to be there when they are in discovery mode. Since many of these perspectives change through conversations with market influencers, we must also identify, understand, and guide these influencers.

As we reach out to individual buyers—whether to invite them to an upcoming event, share some new research or insights, or, as sales people, to engage them regarding what a purchase might look like—we do so with an understanding of where they are in their own unique buying cycle, and how we can help guide them to the next step.

Our accurate understanding of buyers and their online behavior allows us also to see the effect of marketing and sales efforts more holistically than ever before. Looking at an overall revenue funnel, with an understanding of both the value of a lead at any stage and the effect of a marketing campaign at moving leads from one stage to another, we begin to see a truly accurate measurement of our marketing efforts.

As we measure our ability to guide prospects through their individual buying processes, we begin to see the flow of revenue that we can reasonably expect. This predictive approach can also show where in the funnel we're experiencing the biggest leakage of revenue.

By identifying these leaks or inefficiencies, we see the overall awareness, perception, or solution gaps that cause this inefficiency. By responding, either by addressing solution gaps, engaging in conversations that resolve negative perceptions, sharing ideas and perspectives with influencers, or nurturing early-stage buyers to guide their perceptions, we ensure that a steady and predictable flow of revenue moves through the funnel. This way of thinking will be increasingly necessary as the buying landscape continues to change at a furious pace.

This rapid change in the buying landscape is driven mainly by the changing tools accessible to buyers. Each innovation in technology, communication, social relations, or information access has the potential to change buying behavior.

New Devices

Each time a new hardware device enters the market and becomes popular, it has a significant chance of changing buyer access to information—and, thus, how they move through a buying process. Apple's iPhone and iPad, RIM's Blackberry, Google's Android, and other smartphones are clearly changing the buying landscape. Whether any particular device succeeds or not is immaterial. The reality is that we are seeing increasingly functional, interactive, and connected devices every year—and each one that succeeds has a major impact.

Some of the following transitions may be worth thinking about as each new generation of device enters the market:

Returning Relevance of Print Media

Tablet form-factor devices, such as the Kindle, Nook, and iPad are shaking up the print landscape for newspapers and other periodicals. If they succeed, we will see subscribers transition their attention to the mobile environment. This, and the increased targeting precision that comes with it, mean that print advertising, long too untargeted to be a mainstay of B2B marketing, may become increasingly relevant. With pay-for-performance price models and highly precise targeting, advertising opportunities may be as interesting to B2B marketers as search engines were five years ago.

Integration of Offline and Online Experiences

Thinner, lighter form factors make it possible to have more-capable devices with you at all times. For B2B marketers at offline events (e.g. seminars and tradeshows), this means that the online and offline experiences can be melded seamlessly. A salesperson carrying a connected, full-form-factor device can easily segue to a live demonstration if the conversation goes that way. A prospect carrying such a device can be guided to online resources during the booth conversation. The integrated experience can be much greater than either alone, and business buyers are likely to be among the first regular users.

Books and Whitepapers Become Interactive

As books and whitepapers are increasingly read on digital, connected devices, we can leverage rich interactive aspects. Embedded videos within a book, links for more detailed exploration of topics, and interactive experiences to highlight key points all become possible, allowing us to rethink the book and whitepaper formats entirely.

Location Awareness

Most, if not all, new devices include built-in GPS functionality. As they become location-aware, more applications will be re-factored to take advantage of that location knowledge. From Foursquare to Facebook, applications will build-in deep location knowledge of people in your network, allowing new forms of social networking to increasingly bridge the physical divide.

Similarly, this might enable more accurate location-based message targeting and may revive the local breakfast or lunch event as it becomes easier to connect with only local executives.

Application Explosion

The prevalence of mobile and tablet devices, most of which come with robust development and application ecosystems, may mean a great opportunity for "freemium" applications that help prospective buying executives self-educate on the business case for your full solution by experiencing a key aspect of it firsthand.

Sales Enablement Enrichment

On the internal front, field salespeople are also likely candidates to adopt these new devices. Their ability to remain productive and mobile while working with a full-size device means their need for insights and data on leads will greatly increase. Rather than just wanting the name and phone number of a lead sent to their mobile device, they will insist on rich/deep activity data and greater insights—right on the mobile device.

Each change in the device landscape brings the opportunity for significant change in the way our buyers interact with us and discover and absorb information. While each hardware trend may take a few years to fully play out, the hardware devices' effects on buyers are significant enough that they are well worth watching.

New Software

If any trend has dominated the marketing landscape over the last decade, it's the speed with which software platforms are formed, grow to millions or hundreds of millions of users, and then sink into oblivion. As this book goes to print, Twitter, Facebook, and LinkedIn are big, while Friendster, MySpace, and Second Life have passed their primes. As you read this book, a new cast of software platforms is likely ready to dominate the landscape.

Each platform, however, can be understood using the same paradigm and framework for how people acquire information, share perspectives, influence and are influenced by peers, and learn about what is possible. As marketers, we must look at each new platform within this framework and assess the following:

- **Audience:** Who actively uses the platform? Do they fit any of the roles in your buying group: users, technical buyers, economic buyers, or coaches?

- **Influencers:** If direct buyers are not present in significant numbers on the new platform, are there influencers/champions? Is there an opportunity to connect with, and build deeper relationships with, influencers on that platform?

- **Context:** What is the context of the platform? Is it typically used for sharing fun and social information or for discussing business challenges? What is the etiquette of interaction?

- **Conversation:** How are conversations held? One-to-one? Group? Public? Given the context and the audience, what makes sense in terms of selectively joining conversations or engaging with people on the platform?

Also, within any given platform, its usefulness, etiquette, and usage patterns almost certainly evolve as adoption spreads. As marketers, we must approach each platform with an open mind and attempt to understand, through experimentation, how it fits into our revenue engine.

Shared Data, Shared Identities

Another ongoing development worth watching is the evolution of data providers. As we attempt to discern buyer intentions across a lengthy and complex buying process, our ability to understand interactions across many separate systems is key. Tying together interactions in each environment means we must build an understanding of identities that spans platforms.

The most likely approach here is still unclear because it could be done directly by marketers, provided through a data service, or built into a shared identity platform. However, the need to understand buyer interactions across varied media platforms will certainly drive the development of this common view.

Deeper Understanding of Influence

We're also seeing continuous advancement in measuring influence. Understanding exactly how much influence any individual has, on what topics, and with whom, is increasingly measurable. As we list and categorize the people we connect with, follow, and listen to, and as each interaction becomes measureable, we start to understand much more precisely how ideas are transmitted and absorbed through influencers.

As marketers, this has tremendous value, because we can focus on the influencers who can spread ideas or alter perceptions in the key market areas that matter most. A clearer understanding of interests and influences also lets us focus more on our ability to enable messages to be passively discovered with the same precision we find in today's search engines.

The value is clear to major players in the online space, from the search engines and social networking sites, to advertising networks and data providers. Significant investments are underway to enable marketers to leverage this insight, and it's reasonable to expect that this will play a much more important role in marketing in the next few years.

Natural Understanding

As we learn more about the sources affecting lead flow within our revenue engines, another technology can potentially deepen this understanding. Natural language algorithms attempt to understand what is meant in written words, instead of simple keywords. Although still in its early days, natural language technology can potentially enable us to understand, on a large scale, the sentiment toward our offerings within any given audience. This will allow a more rigorous analysis of whether conversations about our products and services are going well, or whether we need to be better understood, corrected, or responded to.

Similarly, natural language algorithms may partly begin to solve the information concierge challenge discussed earlier. Often, a buyer looks for solutions to a certain problems, but doesn't do so in a way that allows the solution to be easily found. Natural language technologies may open up new ways of presenting results that are based on a more intuitive understanding of what he might be interested in, rather than simply the exact keywords used in the search.

THE REVENUE PROCESS

Over time, the importance of understanding, analyzing, and facilitating how prospects buy will outweigh the internal differences between the marketing and sales departments. Each role is, and will remain, crucial. Some professionals will focus on the broader communications that marketing traditionally focuses on and other professionals will focus on the one-to-one interactions now common in the sales organization. However, the interdependence and coordination will only increase as competitive advantage is gained through better buyer understanding and facilitation.

Forward thinking businesses will begin to think of the revenue creation process—the revenue engine itself—as a single, holistic part of the business. Over time, it may even be managed by a single executive responsible for both functions.

The Chief Revenue Officer

The Chief Revenue Officer will be the person who understands, invests in, and optimizes the overall process by which buyers discover, learn, and buy. However, this individual will look very different to today's sales and marketing leaders. He or she will need to recognize that in just the past 10 years, the way buyers buy has shifted dramatically.

The CRO will need to map and model an accurate overall buying process, and understand where each individual is within it. She will need to understand what awareness, perception, or solution challenges prevent people from moving through the funnel, and where those challenges originate. She will need to allocate budgets—in hard dollars, effort, and permission—to address challenges and facilitate buyers as they move through the process.

Some of these efforts may look like classic marketing campaigns and some may involve the traditional personal interactions typical of sales efforts. But the key is:

they are all part of one integrated process. The CRO will need to present the current value of the revenue funnel to the executive team and provide an understanding of how the investments being made are driving its growth.

The Chief Revenue Officer will run the revenue engine.